Parsons
Using part-
time faculty
DATE DUE effectively

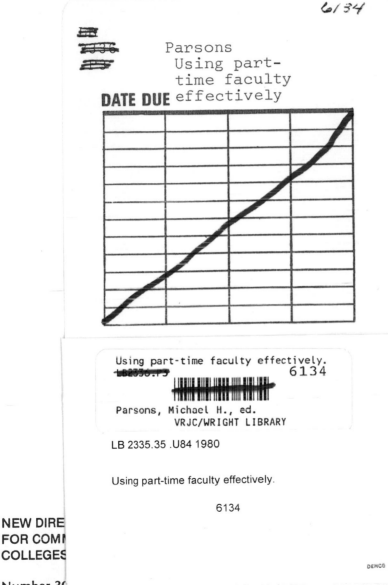

NEW DIRE
FOR COMM
COLLEGES

Number 30   -   1980

NEW DIRECTIONS FOR COMMUNITY COLLEGES

A Quarterly Sourcebook
Arthur M. Cohen, Editor-in-Chief
Florence B. Brawer, Associate Editor
Sponsored by the ERIC Clearinghouse for Junior Colleges

Number 30, 1980

Using Part-Time
Faculty Effectively

Michael H. Parsons
Guest Editor

Jossey-Bass Inc., Publishers
San Francisco • Washington • London

EDUCATIONAL RESOURCES INFORMATION CENTER

ERIC Clearinghouse For Junior Colleges

UNIVERSITY OF CALIFORNIA, LOS ANGELES

USING PART-TIME FACULTY EFFECTIVELY
New Directions for Community Colleges
Volume VIII, Number 2, 1980
 Michael H. Parsons, Guest Editor

New Directions for Community Colleges (publication number 0195-2269)
is published quarterly by Jossey-Bass Inc., Publishers, in association
with the ERIC Clearinghouse for Junior Colleges. Subscriptions are
available at the regular rate for institutions, libraries, and agencies
of $30 for one year. Individuals may subscribe at the special
professional rate of $18 for one year. *New Directions* is numbered
sequentially — please order extra copies by sequential number.
The volume and issue numbers above are included for the
convenience of libraries.

The material in this publication was prepared pursuant to a
contract with the National Institute of Education, U.S.
Department of Health, Education, and Welfare. Contractors
undertaking such projects under government sponsorship are
encouraged to express freely their judgment in professional
and technical matters. Prior to publication, the manuscript
was submitted to the Maryland Council of Community College
Academic Deans for critical review and determination of
professional competence. This publication has met such
standards. Points of view or opinions, however, do not
necessarily represent the official view or opinions of the
Maryland Council of Community College Academic Deans.

Correspondence:
Subscriptions, single-issue orders, change of address notices,
undelivered copies, and other correspondence should be sent to
New Directions Subscriptions, Jossey-Bass Inc., Publishers,
433 California Street, San Francisco, California 94104.
Editorial correspondence should be sent to the Editor-in-Chief,
Arthur M. Cohen, at the ERIC Clearinghouse for Junior Colleges,
University of California, Los Angeles, California 90024.

Library of Congress Catalogue Card Number LC 79-92020

Cover design by Willi Baum

Manufactured in the United States of America

 This publication was prepared with funding from the National Institute of
Education, U.S. Department of Health, Education, and Welfare under
contract no. 400-78-0038. The opinions expressed in the report do not
necessarily reflect the positions or policies of NIE or HEW.

Contents

Editor's Notes

The 1980s will not be an easy decade for America's two-year colleges. Gone are the days of burgeoning enrollments, financial surpluses, and complacent faculties and student bodies. Today the challenge is meeting the needs of the new client by using nontraditional methods and the same or fewer resources. One strategy which has emerged in response to this challenge is staff development. Volumes have been written about its utility in providing self-renewal for faculties, classified staffs, and administrators. Little has been written about its use with part-time (adjunct) faculty.

Why part-time faculty? Recent statistics reveal that over fifty percent of the teachers in today's two-year colleges are part-time. The reasons are obvious: part-time personnel cost less to employ than full-time, bring more diverse and current expertise to the classroom, and are more malleable in adjusting to the temporal, spatial, and design needs of college programming. However, there are hazards in using part-time faculty.

In an era of consumerism, colleges must ensure that the instruction being provided by part-time faculty is commensurate with that provided by full-time faculty. New students may develop impressions of the college based solely on contact with part-time personnel. Can we afford to rely on chance to assure that parity of instruction exists?

This volume of *New Directions for Community Colleges* proposes that colleges realize part-time faculty potential through staff development. The volume is divided into three sections. In the first, an action agenda for staff development is outlined. Carol Eliason, from her program development perspective at American Association of Community and Junior Colleges (AACJC), outlines the problems inherent in current staff development practices. She proposes a systems approach to engaging and solving these problems. David Harris voices concerns from the perspective of the college president and articulates the challenges which must be met. Richard Smith explains how he prepares community college teachers by designing participatory programs which develop the potential of part-time faculty. His chapter is a model for achieving teaching effectiveness. Jack Friedlander has analyzed the results of two national surveys of teaching practices in community colleges and indicates that part-time teachers differ from full-time ones in instructional practices. He suggests that if part-time personnel are to provide the same quality of instruction as full-time, sound staff development programs must be instituted.

The second section presents four models of staff development for part-time faculty. Harmon Pierce and Rosemary Miller describe the program at Burlington County College, a large urban institution. The program design presupposes the support systems that are associated with larger colleges. The chapter by Michael Parsons outlines the operation of the staff development program at Hagerstown Junior College. The components of this program are designed to be used in a smaller institution where support systems are minimal. The program's value is its cost/benefit impact. Richard Greenwood describes a program operating at a medium-sized institution. He has implemented a series of activities that develop a sense of participation in the life of the college by the part-time faculty. Again, many of the activities can be implemented at modest cost. Edward Decker analyzes the challenges faced by those colleges whose staff is predominantly part-time. While his concerns may appear theoretical for most institutions, they have been described by some pundits as the direction of the future.

The third section encompasses areas of concern not covered by the foregoing models. The role of the state in the operation of community colleges in the 1980s is viewed, generally, in negative terms. Joseph P. DeSantis designed a state support system for working with part-time faculty. He advances the design as a positive dimension of state/college interaction and an effective means of staff development. Louis S. Albert and Rollin J. Watson attack the most difficult aspects of working with part-time faculty. If we are going to successfully "mainstream" part-time personnel, we must pay close attention to current legal and administrative issues. Albert and Watson present a plan of action that should become operating procedure at all colleges. The last chapter examines part-time-faculty development from a different perspective. Richard R. Beman, a practicing "adjunct," convincingly tells about the rewards and frustrations of the role. His insights are useful as we seek to develop the potential of part-time faculty in the 1980s.

No sourcebook is a singular effort. A special word of praise is due to my fellow practitioners who took time from their busy schedules to write for this volume. Also, several individuals made special contributions to the project beyond the chapters herein, namely: Richard E. Wilson and N. Carol Eliason of AACJC, Arthur M. Cohen of UCLA,

Atlee C. Kepler, president of Hagerstown Junior College, and Sandy Krieger, secretary and editor.

Michael H. Parsons
Guest Editor

*Michael H. Parsons is dean of instructional affairs at
Hagerstown Junior College. He has been involved
with part-time-faculty development for a decade.*

Community colleges in the 1980s are faced with changing clientele, shrinking resources, and stable instructional staffs. The challenge is to engage society's changing educational needs with systematic approaches to institutional management. Part-time faculty are an important part of the system.

Part-Time Faculty: A National Perspective

N. Carol Eliason

The part-time faculty member has become an unwilling pawn in an increasingly complex chess match being waged on the campuses of America's two-year colleges. To the chair of a burgeoning evening business program, the community's part-timers are viewed as "saviors." To the full-time faculty's chief negotiator, the itinerant part-timer may be perceived as villain in the struggle to save jobs from the retrenchment-minded administrator's ax. Administrators from Oregon to Florida are searching for a magic formula to use in developing workable management planning strategies to meet the strains of double-digit inflation, shrinking appropriations, and a sharp downturn in traditional sixteen to twenty-one-year-old enrollees and a rise in adult part-time students.

According to reports from approximately 1,230 two-year institutions, in October 1978 there were 208,831 faculty employed in these

Statistics for this chapter, unless otherwise credited, were furnished by Fontelle Gilbert, data office associate, American Association of Community and Junior Colleges.

2

institutions including a total of 200,213 in public two-year colleges and 8,618 in independent two-year colleges. The total number of faculty teaching both full-time and part-time in all two-year colleges increased by 4 percent from October 1977 to October 1978, rising from 199,591 to 208,831.

The number of students attending these colleges part time has increased, and the total enrollment, full time and part time, at public and private two-year colleges decreased slightly from 4,309,984 in October 1977 to 4,304,058 in October 1978. Faculty teaching part time increased from fall 1974 when 50 percent were employed part time to fall 1978 when the proportion increased to 57 percent. Of all part-time faculty members in postsecondary institutions 52.6 percent are employed in two-year colleges.

Economic Benefits from Part-Time Faculty

Friedlander (1979) urges hiring even larger numbers of part-time faculty to save major institutional dollars for other purposes — part-timers are seldom compensated at a rate based on credentials and experience. The usual scales are half the standard hourly/credit rates offered full-time faculty. Average salaries for faculty who are teaching full time on a nine-to-ten-month contract in two-year colleges, according to National Center for Education Statistics, was $17,110 for the 1977–78 academic year. Compensation levels for full-time faculty in postsecondary education increased by 5.9 percent from 1976–1977 to 1977–1978. During the same period, the cost-of-living rose by 7.1 percent. Increases for part-timers did not keep pace with either increases in full-time compensation or the cost-of-living.

For public two-year colleges, faculty teaching full-time on a nine-to-ten-month contract earn an average of $17,360; at private two-year colleges the average is $12,840. An assistant professor with a salary of $17,880 would need an increase of 14 percent, or $2,497 to achieve a 1972–73 level of real compensation.

Part-timers are seldom offered health insurance, retirement, or educational benefits matching those of full-time staff. Only California has opened a path to tenure for part-timers. In an American Council on Education study, it was reported that 47 percent of the public two-year colleges grant tenure to their part-time faculty. In public two-year colleges 56 percent of faculty have tenure status while 50 percent of faculty in private two-year colleges have tenure status.

Deans are able to shave institutional costs by reducing the support services and facilities available to part-time staff. Most frequent complaints offered by part-timers are the absence of: (1) facilities and resources for student advisement, (2) clerical and reproduction services, (3) budgets for support media and materials.

Market analysis has proven to knowledgeable academic planners that a well screened pool of qualified community-based instructors and counselors can offer increased flexibility in curriculum and site scheduling. Education is big business today and competition and enrollment changes force institutions to re-examine long cherished planning and staffing tenets.

Profile of Part-Time Students

The number of part-time students is also increasing. Between 1970 and 1977, the proportion of learners aged fourteen to nineteen fell from 36 to 32 percent. About half (45 percent) of the undergraduates in the twenty-five- to thirty-two-year age group were enrolled in two-year colleges. As of October 1977, nearly 1.3 million people, thirty-five or over, were enrolled in college: 60 percent of this population were participating in undergraduate programs, and 80.4 percent were enrolled as part-time students. The proportion of the two-year college learners who were delayed starters (that is, twenty-two- to thirty-four-year olds) enrolled in two-year colleges rose from 31 to 45 percent. In 1970, 53 percent of two-year college learners were under twenty years old; by 1977 this proportion dropped to 37 percent. On the average, part-time learners are older than full-time students. Students twenty-two years old and over have accounted for most of the growth in two-year colleges in the 1970s. Two out of three of these older learners attend part time. National norms for full-time, first-time freshman indicate that 20.4 percent of those enrolled in two-year institutions are from families with incomes of less than $12,500. More learners in two-year colleges are older, married, attending part-time, from less affluent homes, and with parents who have less education than students in four-year colleges and universities. Among two-year college students, 26.7 percent were married and living with their spouses, while 14.3 percent of the four-year college students are married. Of the two-year college students twenty-two and older, 54 percent are married.

Data on college enrollments from the National Longitudinal Study of the High School Class of 1972 reveal that 60 percent of the students initially entering two-year institutions either completed a course of study, transferred to a four-year institution, or were still enrolled two years after college entry. According to the National Center for Education Statistics publication, *Projections of Education Statistics to 1985–86,* two-year institutions are expected to enroll a total of 5.225 million students in the fall of 1980. Between 1965 and 1975, however, two-colleges more than tripled their enrollments, while between 1975 and 1985 enrollment is expected to increase from 3.8 million students to about 5.7 million, an increase of about 50 percent.

Close to half of all students enrolled in two-year colleges are taking courses in occupational-technical fields. Faculty trained in such areas as health technologies, business, data processing, and public service may be in the most demand in the years ahead.

Standards for Part-Time Faculty

Several rural presidents report that part-time faculty is the key to a break-even budget for program startup. In more urban areas deans and institutional researchers have come to view the part-timer as an evangelist who is willing to break into new territories on behalf of the college. It is not uncommon in some of our burgeoning suburbs for new sites to be staffed at night by a seasoned part-time administrator and a cadre of local part-time faculty and counselors. But even if part-time teachers are necessary, can they do the job?

A review of the 1970s literature on part-time faculty problems indicates that there has been continuing concern over the sharp rise in numbers of part-time professional employees. (Bender and Hammons, 1972; Guthrie-Morse, 1979; Lombardi, 1975). Guthrie-Morse notes that the average institution used 88 percent more part-time faculty in 1977 than in 1973. However, little research has been done on cost-effective modes for assuring the student consumer high quality instruction by large numbers of part-time faculty who have only limited commitment to institutional instructional objectives and goals.

Cohen and Brawer (1977) are troubled by a 1975 survey showing lesser teaching experience of part-time humanities faculty. Information from a 1977 AACJC survey indicates that few states require a formal teaching certificate. The requirements are usually slightly different for faculty academic or general education programs than for those teaching in technical fields. Certification requirements for academic faculty often consist of a master's degree in the subject area; for technical fields, the requirement is commonly at least a bachelor's degree, with work experience in the subject area. Although there may be no formal certification requirements, prospective faculty may also be asked for evidence of teaching experience or courses in teaching or education.

In the 1979 AACJC convention forum on part-time faculty needs, it was apparent that there is no clearcut definition of national standards for part-time faculty performance. Some speakers agreed with Jamerson (1979) that "teachers have a responsibility to be committed to the idea of the community college if they choose to be employed by one. Professionalism also requires that they reduce the amount of misinformation and uninformed opinion about the colleges that currently dominates the scene . . . Community College teachers should be trained in programs that not only give them subject matter expertise but also a degree of knowledgeability concerning learning theory, program planning, curricula strategies, evaluation techniques, collective bargaining, educational law and professional ethics" (p. 7). Other speakers argued that the local institutions were forced to take whoever walked in the door and promised to work for "coolie wages."

The part-timer has had several champions (Abel, 1977; Bender and Breuder, 1973; Bender and Hammons, 1972). Each offers insights into the various modes of institutional neglect of one of its richest assets. Among the areas most often cited as in need of change are the multiple wage inequities and hiring practices. Only in California, Maryland, and Illinois has there been a practical attempt to upgrade the skills of part-time faculty.

Little has been done to systematize the orientation, evaluation, retention, and release process outside of the landmark decisions in California and Connecticut. As part of a 1977 decision in Connecticut the State Board of Labor Relations created status and due process for those part-time faculty members who work more than seven and a half hours per week. One protection offered to part-timers working more than seven and a half hours per week was the right to belong to a collective bargaining unit. Yet, most bargaining contracts exclude part-time faculty. The 1979 AACJC interviews with part-time faculty in Michigan, Pennsylvania and New Jersey indicate a growing interest in forming separate collective bargaining units for part-timers. Collective bargaining conflicts between full- and part-time faculty in the same units are intense. Two categories of part-time faculty appear to be most vulnerable to loss of status within large bargaining units composed of part-time and full-time staffs. They are counselors and support staffs from libraries, learning resource centers, and so on, who work on contact hour contracts. More research will be needed to develop equitable remedies to their dilemma.

Tighter controls are inevitable. The question is who will control staff. Guidelines are being developed by regional accrediting associations such as middle states to better monitor institutional staffing practices to assure that there is an institution-wide commitment and that resources are available to meet stated objectives. Bills have been introduced in several legislatures to "cap" enrollments and thus limit state subsidies to institutions. The most stringent of these limitations, those in Massachusetts and Connecticut, are coupled with staffing quotas and formulas.

The courts of Washington, California, and Michigan have ruled on a number of hotly contested issues surrounding the status of part-time faculty. Though definitions of rights, responsibilities, and conditions of employment have been continuously refined during collective bargaining marathons in twenty-odd states during the last decade, several sensitive issues remain. Among those worthy of further scrutiny are:

- Under what conditions are the collective bargaining rights of part-time faculty best served? In units including full-time faculty? In separate units? Outside of collective bargaining?
- How can an institution provide quality instructional services with large numbers of part-timers?
- What are appropriate modes for selection, orientation, monitoring, evaluation, and release for part-timers?
- What kinds of compensation formulas can be devised to better balance institutional fiscal problems against the financial demands of this group of employees? These people are a vital link to community attitudes about the college and its instructional products. If they are treated poorly, they can speedily undo the most sophisticated community or public relations campaign.

Social Benefits from Part-Time Faculty

Although part-time faculty can generally be hired for less money than full-time, it is my own perception, based on a decade of travels to campuses in thirty-five states, that academic supervisors have had at least three additional reasons for hiring part-time faculty. First, part-timers frequently enable administrators to meet affirmative action guidelines by upgrading minority or female employee participation levels. This is especially important when we note that women have become the majority group among all undergraduate learners in the traditional age group of twenty-one or under. Women over thirty-five increased their attendance rate by 5.9 percent between 1974 and 1976. AACJC annual fall enrollment data indicate that women comprise half of the full-time population and over half (52 percent) of the part-time population.

The Carnegie study of women students (Eliason, 1977) found that an overwhelming number of the 1,166 female students felt the need for faculty role models as they pursued skills and credentials for labor market entry or reentry. Though the percentage of women is increasing, approximately two thirds of all faculty members are men. In 1976, women comprised 35 percent of faculty as compared with 37 percent in 1978. If administrators fail to maintain programs and sensitive personnel to staff such programs, institutions are likely to lose the largest single potential-growth population open to recruitment in the 1980s. In times of retrenchment, part-time female faculty hired in the early to mid 1970s have felt the economic pressures of being "last in the door, first out." Because they are seldom covered by workable grievance systems, their problems are poorly documented at this time.

Community colleges enroll 38.8 percent of the nation's minority students. According to a new AACJC minority study, from 1970 to 1978 there was a 52 percent increase in minority enrollment. Black enrollment increased by about 30 percent, and Hispanic enrollment, 65 percent. States with the highest minority enrollment include Hawaii, New Mexico, Alaska, Louisiana, South Carolina, Alabama, California, Texas, Maryland, and Mississippi. During these same years, black faculty increased 55 percent and Hispanic faculty increased 260 percent. There has been small growth for Asians and little or no growth for American Indians.

Second, in the recent past part-time faculty positions offered inexperienced faculty a toehold between graduate training and full employment. For deans this group of employees was a pool of talent for the next expansion year.

Third, in community-based programs part-time faculty have provided a link to local government, community organizations, and industry.

Scarcity of Teaching Positions

Before an institution is ready to use part-time faculty within an overall cost-effective staffing plan, a thorough and open investigation should be made of the institution's reasons for hiring part-time staff. Moreover, the following trends should be noted.

The proportion of faculty teaching full-time (defined as a teaching load of nine hours or more) continues to decrease. In the fall of 1974, 51 percent taught full time. By fall 1978, 43 percent of the faculty taught full time.

Of the part-time faculty who are semi-retired, 44.4 percent are in two-year colleges. This group consists of faculty who have left full-time teaching and faculty who have taught part time during their entire career.

Passage of the Age Discrimination in Employment Act (ADEA) means that after July 1, 1982, mandating retirement before age seventy is illegal. Under this act projected junior faculty openings for all post-secondary education is zero for six years with recovery commencing only after 1988.

Another issue still to be addressed in many institutions is what to do with tenured full-time faculty whose skills are no longer in high demand. Should they be given priority access to teaching slots in programs for which their credentials are second rate at the expense of more competent part-timers?

Occupational outlooks through 1985 indicate that there will be keen competition for both college and university teaching positions because the supply of new master's and doctoral candidates will more than meet the demand.

Cohen and Lombardi (1979) argue that a weighty question for the 1980s seems to be the extent to which community colleges will go in the direction of the three C's—career, compensatory, and community education. Each institution will respond in different ways, but the national trend or curricular demand of the past five years seems to be gaining momentum. The biggest downward enrollment shifts have been in the humanities and social sciences. This means the largest potential faculty casualties appear to be in foreign languages, philosophy, literature, and history. These courses are key elements in college parallel programs. A common occurrence during staff development training across the U.S. this year has been the difficulty of convincing the liberal arts faculty that these changes can be successfully faced through marketing, staff retraining, and nontraditional delivery systems. It is imperative that this group comes to grips with the reality of labor surplus problems 1980's style!

According to the National Center for Education Statistics (NCES), employment of full-time teaching faculty in all postsecondary education will show small growth through 1982 and will then drop by

5.7 percent over the next three-year period. After 1985 no increase can be expected.

Data show that over 75 percent of two-year college faculty have the master's degree and that nearly 14 percent have the doctorate. It is predicted that by 1980 more than 20 percent of these faculty members will either have or be working on the doctoral degree. Data from the Bureau of Labor Statistics indicate there will be more than two Ph.D.-holders for every position requiring a Ph.D.

Community Colleges Must Hire Part-Time Faculty

If the hopes of the future for community colleges are to be managed with equity and economic strategy, planning must gear staffing to better serve adult part-time students. The adult part-time learner will be the largest single growth population in the 1980s. Planners thus must begin to better cope with the knotty problems presented by major fluctuations in staff requirements. The adult who turns to the two-year college for skills and/or credentials needs instant service — community colleges must be ready to provide work skills to match the changing requirements of the job market. A static faculty cannot provide this.

Community colleges will continue to serve youthful populations seeking entry skills. However, administrators who are not planning now to adjust staff requirements to meet shrinking daytime teenage populations may deserve the growing wrath of retrenching former staff unless they heed Hammons' (1979) call for reassessing community college faculty prerequisites and position responsibilities. Hammons emphasizes both are imperatives to assure the student consumer quality instruction. He defines the faculty prerequisites as follows: "the knowledge and skills which should be possessed prior to employment while position responsibilities outline specific tasks which faculty might be expected to perform." The equally important position responsibilities include five basic elements: "(1) teaching which is divided into four parts: preparation, implementation, evaluation, management; (2) advisement to students (3) service to the community; (4) service to the college; (5) personal development" (p. 36–37).

There are some excellent little-known examples of positive institutional responses to managing part-time faculty. Among the best encountered in recent months are:

1. Moraine Valley Community College in Illinois has developed a systems approach to part-time faculty orientation which includes

training sessions at the school and a Part-Time Instructor's Manual. This valuable handbook includes basic facts on college policies, practices, and resources as well as practical tips on advising adult students, adult learning styles, and effective teaching modes. It also invites the part-timers to participate in institutional planning through submission of new course suggestions and narrative evaluation forms.

2. Hagerstown Junior College in Maryland has used a state grant to develop modular print and video materials for all of the state's two-year institutions. A key element is an annual schedule of regionally dispersed topical workshops.

3. The learning resource center of a community college becomes a vital link between institutional policy planners and part-time faculty when it distributes instructional improvement tools. The Alexandria campus of Northern Virginia Community College has a catalog of materials which assists both the novice and the pro to strengthen instructional skills. They even have audio visual tutorial materials for those who instruct Vietnamese refugees.

It is also possible to adapt orientation programs for full-time faculty to serve part-time faculty. For example, California's Cañada College has a semester-long series of hands-on activities to familiarize the new professional employee with all facets of college operations and philosophy. This includes reading, discussions, site visits, and data collection. Full-time faculty are compensated with a reduced teaching load.

Summary

In the 1980s the quest for zero-based budgeting must not halt efforts to improve the quality of instructional services provided by a growing cadre of community college part-time faculty. Through systems approaches to institutional management we can develop an equitable approach to better serving our ever-changing student populations. The price may be high but the rewards will be felt in student and community satisfaction with our educational products.

References

Abel, E. K. "Invisible and Indispensible: Part-Time Teachers in California Community Colleges." *Community/Junior College Research Quarterly,* 1977, *2* (1), 77–91.

Bender, L., and Hammons, J. O. "Adjunct Faculty: Forgotten and Neglected." *Community and Junior College Journal,* 1972, *43* (2), 20–22.

Bender, L. W., and Breuder, R. "Part-Time Teachers—'Step-Children' of the Community College." *Community College Review*, 1973, *1* (1), 29–37.

Cohen, A. M., and Brawer, F. B. *The Two-Year College Instructor Today.* New York: Praeger, 1977.

Cohen, A. M., and Lombardi, J. "Can the Community College Survive Success?" *Change*, 1979, *11* (8), 24–27.

Eliason, C. *Women in Community Colleges.* Washington, D. C.: American Association of Community and Junior Colleges, 1977.

Friedlander, J. "Instructional Practices of Part-Time and Full-Time Faculty." *Community College Review*, 1979, *6* (3), 65–72.

Guthrie-Morse, B. "The Utilization of Part-time Faculty in Community Colleges." *Community College Frontiers*, 1979, *7* (3), 8–17.

Hammons, J. O. "The Multi-Faceted Role of an 'Ideal' CC Faculty Member." *Community College Review*, 1979, *7* (2), 36–41.

Jamerson, F. "The Community College Teacher: A Confused Identity." *Community College Review*, 1979, *7* (3), 4–7.

Leslie, D. W., and Head, R. B. "Part-Time Faculty Rights." *Educational Record*, 1979, *60* (1), 46–67.

Lombardi, J. *Part-Time Faculty in Community Colleges.* Topical Paper No. 54. Los Angeles: ERIC Clearinghouse for Junior Colleges, 1975. ED 115 316.

Further Readings in Part-Time Faculty Development

Cohen, A. M., and Brawer, F. B. *The Two-Year College Instructor Today.* New York: Praeger, 1977.

DeNevi, D. "Retreading Teachers the Hard Way." In *Community College Programs for People Who Need College.* Washington, D.C.: American Association of Junior Colleges, 1970.

Eliason, C. *Neglected Women: The Educational Needs of Displaced Homemakers, Single Parents, and Older Women.* Washington, D.C.: The National Advisory Council on Women's Educational Equity Programs, 1978.

Ferris, P. *The Part-Time Instructor in the Los Rios District: An Analysis.* Sacramento, Calif.: Los Rios Comunity College District. (ED 121 364.)

Grymes, R. J., Jr. *A Survey and Analysis of Part-Time Instructor at J. Sargeant Reynolds Community College.* Richmond, Va.: J. Sargeant Reynolds Community College, 1976. (ED 125 687.)

Harrison, J. D. "Ph.D. Faculty in Community Colleges." *Community College Review*, 1979, *6* (3), 24–28.

Koltai, L. "The Part-Time Faculty and the Community College." An address presented at the Conference on Part-Time Teachers, Inglewood, Calif., January 28, 1976. (ED 118 174.)

National Center for Education Statistics. *Projections of Educational Statistics to 1985–86.* Washington, D.C.: National Center for Education Statistics, 1976.

Sanchez, B. M. "ERIC Clearinghouse for Junior Colleges: Characteristics of Community College Faculty." *Community College Frontiers*, 1979, *7* (3), 54–55.

Sewell, D. H., and others. *Report on a Statewide Survey About Part-Time Faculty in California Community Colleges.* Sacramento: California Community and Junior College Association, 1976. (ED 118 195.)

Wenrich, J., and Eakin, D. J. "Faculty Orientation in Community Colleges." *Community College Review*, 1978, *6* (2), 8–13.

Wilson, R. J., and others. *Colleges Professors and Their Impact on Students.* New York: Wiley, 1975.

*N. Carol Eliason is the project director, Center for Women's
Opportunities, at the American Association of Community
and Junior Colleges. She has been a consultant to
community colleges in thirty-five states.*

*The critical issues surrounding the use of part-time faculty
are enumerated and suggestions for action are advanced.*

From the President's Perspective:
Part-Time Faculty
in the 1980s

David A. Harris

One of the most impressive features of the community college experience has been the use of part-time faculty. They bring to the college a richness and diversity of experience that usually is not found in a full-time faculty. This is especially true is the business and industrial areas, where part-time faculty members can offer up-to-the-minute observations to students who will soon be competing for jobs in the marketplace.

Historically the employment of part-time faculty has reflected the ebbs and flows of societal economic circumstances. During the 1950s, 1960s, and early 1970s, an unusual emphasis was placed upon hiring full-time faculty, with a corresponding decreased emphasis on the role of part-time faculty. Even accrediting agencies looked askance at those colleges having a substantial part-time faculty. During this period, community colleges primarily used part-time faculty when more sections of a course were needed than could be taught by existing full-time faculty. Then, when a sufficient number of additional sections were successfully offered, departmental justification was appended to a request to the administration for additional full-time faculty. Unfortunately, the era of consistent enrollment increases and concomitant expanding resources finally ran its course by the early 1970s.

Presidents were forced to become concerned with the new reality of managing institutions characterized by increasing costs and, allowing for inflation, and fixed or declining dollars. Thus, one of the most impressive challenges encountered by presidents in recent years has been the steady rise in recruitment and use of part-time faculty. Too frequently, the major impetus for this development has been one of sheer economic necessity. That employment of part-time faculty is a money-saving device has been seen as sufficient justification. Perhaps, when one considers the many perplexing problems created by increasing use of part-time faculty, the financial rationale may be viewed as short-sighted.

One immediate problem resulting from this alteration in staffing patterns has been encountered in the recruitment and deployment of part-time faculty members within the institution. Colleges are struggling, with limited success, to identify and implement models that are capable of providing a systematic, rational, and continuous program of part-time faculty recruitment. Across the nation schools are suffering from a lack of administrative expertise at the departmental and divisional level to effectively attract, hire, and retain qualified part-time faculty members. Research and dissemination models must be developed in order to assist colleges in making more rational efforts in this area.

Much has been written about the importance of the part-time faculty to the overall college environment. Less has been written in terms of what motivates part-time faculty members to seek employment with community colleges. And little has been said about their expectations from this employment.

A community college president deals happily with the business executive, the manager, the draftsman, or the expert welder who is enriched by relaying his own expertise to students on a part-time basis. For these faculty members, teaching is an ego-renewing experience. It is also a temporary commitment secondary to a different full-time job. However, presidents deal less easily with the expectations of the graduate teaching assistant, the All But Dissertation history scholar, or the high school teacher, many of whom view their part-time employment as that first critical step toward full-time employment at the college level. In fact, for a considerable number of these faculty members, the main source of money is part-time teaching. This has raised (in California and Michigan) the growing issue of under what circumstances property rights become vested in part-time faculty members. There is a definite need to define legally and state contractually the limits of institutional liability to part-time faculty.

Most part-time faculty are employed during the evening hours. Consequently evening students experience institutional contact through part-time faculty members. Since the part-time faculty member often lacks basic knowledge concerning institutional policies and procedures, problems, ranging from financial aid to career counseling, are either not communicated or are miscommunicated to the students.

Institutions with student populations in excess of 8,000 face a particular problem in managing the large numbers of part-time faculty that are employed within particular divisions. In some cases, it is not unusual to find divisional administrators coping with fifty to eighty part-time faculty members during the session. Increased management resources are essential in such situations.

Because of the lack of appropriate and well-implemented staff development programs, colleges fail to make the most of the diversity offered by part-time faculty. Staff development programs should be mandatory for part-time faculty and institutions should make allowances by contract for part-time faculty involvement. The additional expense, although narrowing the cost advantage vis-a-vis the full-time faculty member, provides a program critical to the successful functioning of the part-time faculty member.

Although there is not a nationally-agreed formula in terms of full-time to part-time faculty ratios, institutions become hard pressed to provide effective management when the number of student credit hours generated by part-time faculty exceeds 30 percent. Thereafter, programs and courses suffer from insufficient full-time faculty in providing for necessary curricula and instructional control.

The vital role played by part-time faculty will withstand the instructional, philosophic, and legal problems. Part-time faculty represent enrichment, diversity, scheduling flexibility, short-term contractual obligations, and a degree of economic savings, but these remain potential until there are functioning recruitment and retention models. Management has a continuing responsibility for recruitment, evaluation, and retention of active part-time faculty members. One way to achieve this is through a strong staff development program, specifically tailored for the needs of the part-time faculty member. But this is not enough — part-time faculty members should understand what the institution expects of them and these expectations should be specified in their contracts. Part-time faculty need to be regarded as valuable institutional resources.

David A. Harris is president of the Florissant Valley Community College in the St. Louis Community College District. He holds the Ph.D. degree in higher education from Michigan State University. Prior to his current position, he has been a community college administrator in four states.

*Part-time faculty are becoming a significant segment of the
resources of community colleges. The time has come to
pool our resources to help part-timers teach effectively.*

Can Participatory Programs
Realize Part-Time
Faculty Potential?

Richard R. Smith

The number of part-time faculty teaching in community colleges has
risen dramatically and community college professionals are not only
challenged but required to assist these teachers as they attempt to edu-
cate students. A 140 percent increase in the use of part-time instructors
from 1971 to 1977 has been reported by Friedlander (1978). During
these years, full-time teachers experienced a 20 percent growth rate.
This change in faculty composition poses problems and questions that
are obvious to all professionals who care about the ability of community colleges to function effectively. Part-time faculty "are becoming
a significant segment of the two-year college's effort — too significant to
ignore if an administration's aim is the continuing enhancement of educational quality and productivity" (Hammons, Wallace, and Watts,
1978, p. 38).

Part-time faculty are asked to enter the classroom and accept
the responsibility to teach while at the same tme they are often encum-
bered by inadequate support systems, lack of understanding of the

philosophy of the community college, inaccurate perception of their students, unclear course syllabi, and little knowledge of alternatives that may be available to them. Many adjunct instructors have never experienced an orientation program that responds to their needs, and they have never had the opportunity to participate in a valid and continuous process of evaluation. The "why" for inservice programs for part-time instructors can be defended. What is difficult to defend is the lack of response to the needs of a growing population of adjunct faculty. In fact, there is no accurate awareness of their needs.

Components for Inservice Programs
for Part-Time Faculty

The increased complexity of the community college and its environment has made it difficult for the part-time instructor to perform effectively. It has been claimed that the historical functions of the community college would be placed in reverse order if viewed in terms of numbers of people being served (Yarrington, 1979). Community colleges are increasingly responding to community demands, often resulting in hiring highly specialized part-time instructors. If the simultaneous moves toward increased state control and dwindling fiscal supports (the most frequently cited reason for increased hiring of part-timers) are considered, it is possible that faculty members might experience a weakening of a group-sense of professional solidarity (Johnston, 1979). This would be devastating—it is critical that both part-time and full-time instructors be aware of the issues facing the community college so they may serve. Therefore, the effectiveness of inservice programs for adjunct instructors will depend upon the programs' philosophical base and their relationship to community college priorities.

Part-time faculty frequently bring a specialized level of skill and knowledge into the community college classroom which the full-time faculty cannot provide. When asking if part-time instructors are as effective as full-time instructors and if staff development programs work for part-time staff, Moe (1977) stated that "the available information provides no definitive answers but does suggest some directions for policy makers and planners" (p. 36). Moe conducted a survey in 1975 and concluded that the most common inservice activities for part-time instructors were designed to help them adjust to the college and learn about requirements; few opportunities were given to improve their teaching.

A five-phase model for adjunct-faculty development was presented by Parsons (1977). The five phases are recruitment, orientation, communication, support services, and evaluation. He recommended the formation of a search committee to coordinate recruitment activities since "without a procedure, a college relies on chance. The result, too often, is a mediocre instructor and a dissatisfied student" (p. 2). The orientation phase involves meeting with the division chairperson to review text materials, course syllabus, and sample tests. This is followed by discussion of a part-time faculty handbook and participation in an adjunct faculty workshop. Continued communication was considered essential since benefits derived from prior developmental activities will be lost by failure to maintain contact with adjunct instructors. Parsons (1977) maintains that "adjunct faculty require the same auxiliary services as the regular faculty if they are to function effectively" (p. 5). The model works because both sides participate—the college evaluates the part-time instructor's teaching and the adjunct has the opportunity to critique the services he is receiving.

It is obvious that Union College agrees with the emphasis Parsons has placed on the importance of maintaining communication with part-time instructors. Union College encouraged the adjunct faculty to organize itself so that it could be represented in discussions with the administration (Orkin, 1979). Although not a bargaining unit, the organization does provide a chance to discuss with administration concerns specific to part-time instructors such as seniority, preference in assignments, and compensation.

A total of 326 two-year colleges responded to a survey (Centra, 1976) conducted to determine faculty development practices in colleges and universities in the United States. The respondents tended to cite practices related to teaching improvement when asked to select practices that were both little or not at all used yet viewed as "essential to faculty development" (p. 24). The responses from each institution were analyzed and grouped according to patterns of estimated use. The practices of availability of specialists "to assist individual faculty in instructional or course development" and to provide "assistance to the faculty in improving teaching skills" were seen as important aids to instructors (p. 48). Practices intended to improve teaching should be available to part-time instructors.

The primary function of part-time instructors in the community college is to teach effectively and to do this, they must be able to answer student questions related to subject matter content and college policies. This recognition prompted Hammons, Wallace, and Wats (1978) to recommend several techniques that may be useful helping part-timers assimilate the information necessary to respond to those questions. They viewed the publication of an adjunct faculty handbook and the development of a mentor system as two low-cost effective techniques. They stressed that adjunct faculty need to know the college is interested in their work and the institution is concerned with both instructional improvement and professional growth. A fourth suggestion focused on evaluation and inservice training activites. Instructional evaluation procedures should be as similar as possible to those experienced by full-time faculty, with emphasis on instructional and professional growth rather than simply determining if the adjunt professor should be rehired. Part-time instructors could be invited to attend insevice programs for full-time faculty or be paid to attend programs specifically designed to respond to their needs.

Educators have grappled with the question of how the university can best bring about instructional change in the community college. Schultz (1977, p. 62) asked "how should the university's commitment be carried out in the future?" He concluded that scholarly activity and research should be a major part of the effort of the university. That conclusion seems appropriate when considering that research on the instructional impact of many of the inservice practices mentioned had not yet been conducted (Friedlander, 1978).

Cooperative Programs for Part-Time Instructors

Needs-Assessment. When exploring cooperative potentials between institutions, many hard realities (such as, role, need, funding, staff reciprocity, and motivation) must be dealt with. The project staff of the University of Illinois had to face some of those issues (Kozoll and others, 1978) when the Illinois Office of Education awarded the Department of Vocational and Technical Education and the Office of Continuing Education and Public Service a grant to develop inservice programs for part-time instructors at Illinois Central College, Lake Land College, and Richland Community College. The project staff assessed the needs of the 500 part-time instructors at those three community colleges. The priorities identified were the need for communication with administrators and other full and part-time faculty, better preparation for teaching, better methods to assess student motivation and needs, increased competence in counseling students, and staff and support services. The needs-assessment was conducted by the project staff in cooperation with the colleges. Thereafter, the staff's "role shifted to diagnosis, encouragement, and suggestions for alternative courses of action" (p. 11).

After the needs-assessment was completed, each community college developed its own inservice program for part-timers. There were some common elements, however. All three colleges designated an individual to be responsible for project programs and services and they all organized an ongoing advisory committee of part-time faculty. Whatever their methods, the programs provided an opportunity for adjuncts to communicate with their supervisors, discuss courses and syllabi with full-time faculty, receive assistance with instructional or counseling problems, and become aware of the role of the community college and the value of their contributions.

Handbook. The literature frequently recommends the development of a handbook for part-time instructors. Weichenthal and others (1977) described a five-section handbook they prepared for the three Illinois colleges mentioned earlier. The handbook's concept was that staff development for part-time faculty is a three-stage process. The first stage is orientation. The second focuses on instructional effectiveness for part-timers who have taught one to three terms and the third stage concentrates on maintaining the motivation of part-time faculty who have taught more than three terms.

Graduate Courses and Internships. The type of cooperative endeavor for faculty development varies from project to project. Community colleges and universities can work together so that the program and faculty needs of each can be served. As an example, Virginia Polytechnic Institute and State University (VPI and SU) worked with the administrators and faculty of New River Community College (NRCC) to plan a long-range program for instructional improvement which included the provision of formal graduate course offerings for full- and part-time faculty on the NRCC campus. NRCC urged adjunct faculty to participate through a program of tuition reimbursement. The university also served as consultants to NRCC for master planning and presentation of specialized workshops. At the same time VPI and SU relied on NRCC as a demonstration center for its community college education program. Teaching and administrative interns were placed at NRCC while NRCC faculty and administrators served as guest lecturers at VPI and SU (Atwell and Sullins, 1973). The faculty of VPI and SU continue to participate in the presentation of inservice programs for adjunct faculty at many community colleges.

More Than One School or State. It is also possible for more than one community college to join forces with one or more universities to offer a professional development program for faculty members. In Texas the Tarrant County Junior College District and the Dallas Community College District joined forces to enable personnel to pursue graduate studies from one of seven universities (Miller, 1974). The New Jersey Consortium on the Community College, Inc., (NJCCC) initiated its statewide faculty and staff development program during the 1976–77 academic year. Further, efforts have not been confined to community colleges within a single state. The NJCCC in cooperation with the Pennsylvania Commission for Community Colleges offered a Conference on Part-Time Faculty to address topics pertinent to adjuncts. The conference was underwritten by a grant from the Fund for the Improvement of Postsecondary Education to promote cooperation between the community colleges of New Jersey and Pennsylvania (Annual Report of Professional Development, 1977).

Inservice Institutes. Taking a slightly different emphasis, Burlington County College (BCC) has viewed the overall goal of faculty development to be improvement of student learning. This commitment has been translated into a series of inservice institutes for part-time faculty. Adjunct participants are not only paid to complete the work and attend the sessions, but completion of the institute is a prerequisite for higher pay and advancement to senior faculty status (Pierce, 1976). BCC and Rutgers University have worked together to provide a development opportunity for all faculty by offering a sequence of graduate courses on the campus of BCC that can lead to a Certificate in Higher Education Studies awarded by the university. Rutgers has also offered graduate courses on the campuses of Bergen, Mercer, and Essex Community Colleges.

Formal Degree Programs. The cooperation works both ways. Community college professionals can and should serve as advisors to universities and four-year colleges in their attempts to provide formal programs of graduate study for staff development and preservice purposes. Each type of institution can act as a resource to the other. Glassboro State College, a four-year school, offers a Master of Arts Program in junior college teaching within which a candidate may select one of eight teaching specialization areas. Part of the program is an advisory council with representatives from seven area community colleges appointed by their presidents. All students must complete a supervised internship at a cooperating college. The goals of the degree candidates are varied. In the beginning the program primarily prepared students to teach at the community college, but more recently an increased number of candidates have entered the program for professional development or to prepare themselves to teach part time in the community college. Community college administrators and faculty have frequently taught in the program.

Workshops. Continuous communication between Glassboro and the area community colleges has resulted in offering courses, workshops, or seminars on the campuses of Atlantic, Burlington, Cumberland, Gloucester, and Salem County Colleges. Instructors have been drawn from the faculty ranks of Glassboro, the community colleges, and Rutgers. Faculty from the community colleges and Glassboro have teamed together to offer workshops at regional and national conferences. These cooperative endeavors seek the resolution of issues or the creation of materials and policies that have direct impact on part-time instructors. In March 1979 Gloucester County College sponsored a Career Development Day and invited its own part- and full-time faculty and the faculty members of every community college in the state of New Jersey. Gloucester offered to pay partial travel expenses. Small and large group sesions were scheduled with contributors representing seven community colleges, Glassboro State College, and Rutgers University.

The Institute of Higher Education Research and Services of the University of Alabama also offers workshops and conferences to community colleges on such topics as the improvement of instruction and faculty development. The programs are scheduled to accommodate part-time community college instructors who have been invited to attend. (Institute of Higher Education Research and Services, 1977).

The variations on the theme of cooperation are many. It is apparent that the interests of community colleges, state colleges, universities, consortia, and institutes often coincide. At a time when the freedom to develop new resources to respond to new demands is limited, there is no choice but to better use existing resources to improve the effectiveness of part-time instructors. Cooperation has proved it can do this.

Prognosis for Participation

Educators must recognize that the goal is student achievement. This statement implies that students who participate in a formal program of study have every right to expect that the best possible resources are available to them when they study in community colleges. If an increased number of part-time instructors is seen as an encumbrance, there must be an aggressive response to that perception. To date the response had been to encumber both the student and the part-time instructor. If the basic goal is to promote student learning, the first step is to face the issue of how to help adjunct faculty improve the quality of their instruction.

It is time to recognize that the growing number of part-time instructors need at least the same supports as full-timers. It is up to the community colleges to give students and adjuncts a chance to achieve. Full-time faculty are typically afforded that opportunity by state and local mandate.

The obligation to consciously design and implement inservice programs to help part-timers increase their teaching effectiveness cannot be said too often. Teaching is their primary function as employees of the community college. The present problems of increased costs, community expectations, and the "species specifics" of technical and occupational requirements present problems that are so complex, we are required to provide a conceptual response.

It is no longer possible to spend all the teaching budget for a full-time faculty. The numbers of part-timers are growing—they must be brought into the group. This is difficult in times of fiscal limitation. The community college can either bring them directly into the existing group or it can tailor additional incentives and programs for part-time teachers. Although that decision is the prerogative of each college, it must be dealt with. An obvious option is to join forces. Cooperation is easy to talk about but difficult to initiate and maintain. Cooperation must operate within a program that offers equality for everyone involved. This means walking the tightrope between homogeneity and institutional uniqueness. It also means preserving the integrity of all cooperating institutions while being willing to share resources. If a community college can view a cooperative endeavor as serving itself while helping others, it may be more successful in obtaining the commitment of the total institution. It is necesssary for each college to develop an institutional ideal, an attitude that by helping others grow, it helps itself. Community colleges can no longer function in isolation. They must grow together by pooling resources to help part-timers teach more effectively. There are common liabilities; if all schools extend themselves to share resources, in the long run they will share the rewards. The approach, from state to state and college to college can be eclectic in organization but it must be uniform in intent.

The participation of universities, consortia, industry, state colleges, and community colleges must be clearly articulated if a sense of commitment and trust are to exist. A basic challenge is to break the barrier of self-sufficiency and free all to share the unique resources of each. Each institution has its purpose; each has its fit in a cooperative endeavor. Assuming the existence of participating inservice programs, the prognosis is that students will benefit from cooperation committed to developing the potentials of part-time faculty.

References

Atwell, C. A., and Sullins, R. W. "Cooperative Faculty Development." *Community and Junior College Journal,* 1973, *44* (3), 32–33.

Centra, J. A. *Faculty Development Practices in U.S. Colleges and Universities.* Princeton, N.J.: Educational Testing Service, 1976.

Friedlander, J. "Using the Talents of Part-Time Faculty." *ERIC Junior College Resource Review,* 1978, pp. 3–6.

Hammons, J., Wallace, T. H., and Watts, G. *Staff Development in the Community College: A Handbook.* Topical Paper No. 66. Los Angeles: ERIC Clearinghouse for Junior Colleges, June 1978.

Institute of Higher Education Research and Services. *IHERS: Purposes and Programs.* University: University of Alabama, 1977.

Johnston, J. R. "From the Editor's Desk." *Community College Frontiers,* 1979, *7* (3), 2–3.

Kozoll, C. E., and others. "Staff and Organization Development. An Analysis of Their Interaction in a Community College Setting and Resulting Changes." Paper prepared for the Adult Education Research Conference, San Antonio, Texas, April 1978. (ED 152 989)

Miller, B. W. "Graduate Career Development Center for Community College Personnel." *Audiovisual Instruction,* 1974, *19* (1), 21.

Moe, J. "A Staff Development Model for Part-Time Instructors." In T. O'Banion (Ed.), *New Directions for Community Colleges: Developing Staff Potential,* no. 19. San Francisco: Jossey-Bass, 1977.

New Jersey Consortium on the Community College. *Professional Development.* Annual report (1976–1977) of the New Jersey Consortium on the Community College, August 1977.

Orkin, S. Letter from President of Union College, October 19, 1979.

Parsons, M. H. "To Right the Unrightable Wrong . . . A Five-Phase Model for Adjunct Faculty Development, New Jersey Consortium on the Community College, Cherry Hill, N.J., December 7, 1977.

Pierce, H. B. "Adjunct (Part-Time) Faculty." In C. Case (Ed.), *Staff Development for the Five Clienteles: Readings on Community College Staff Development Programs for New Faculty, Experienced Faculty, Adjunct (Part-Time) Faculty, Classified Staff and Management.* Pittsburg, Calif.: Community College Press, 1976.

Schultz, R. E. "The University as an Agent of Instructional Change in Community Colleges." In J. O. Hammons (Ed.), *New Directions for Community Colleges: Changing Instructional Strategies,* no. 17. San Francisco: Jossey-Bass, 1977.

Weichenthal, P. B., and others. *Professional Development Handbook for Community College Part-Time Faculty Members.* Urbana: College of Education and Office of Continuing Education and Public Services, University of Illinois, 1977. (ED 156 288)

Yarrington, R. "Directions for Lifelong Learning for the Remainder of the Century." Paper (draft) presented at the National Conference on Total Institutional Response to the Lifelong Learner, Utica, N.Y., March 9, 1979.

*Richard R. Smith is a professor in the Department of
Educational Administration at Glassboro State
College. He also serves as Coordinator of
the Master of Arts Program in Junior
College Teaching.*

Part-time faculty differ from full-time on most measures
related to instructional practices.

Instructional Practices
of Part-Time Faculty

Jack Friedlander

A question that has been the subject of much debate is whether hiring part-time instructors instead of full-time instructors contributes to or detracts from the quality of a community college's educational programs. The answer to this question is particularly important since over 55 percent of the instructors in two-year colleges are now employed part-time (American Association of Community and Junior Colleges, 1979).

Arguments advanced in support of hiring part-time instead of full-time faculty are based on three premises. The first is that colleges can save substantial sums of money by using adjunct rather than regular instructors. Part-timers paid on an hourly rate typically receive from one third to one half the salary paid full-timers who teach the same courses (Lombardi, 1975). Additional savings are realized by most community colleges by not paying part-time teachers for course-related activities that take place outside the classroom (class preparation, office hours, attendance at departmental meetings, participation in professional development activities) and excluding them from receiving fringe benefits, salary increases, and the right to earn security of employment.

The second premise for employing part-time instructors is that the college can thus increase its curriculum and scheduling flexibility. It can hire faculty with special skills for regular and non-traditional courses that the full-time faculty are not prepared to teach; schedule classes in off-campus locations at a variety of times (evenings, weekends); and use part-timers to staff courses where success in terms of enrollments is uncertain, thus providing administrators with the option of cancelling the courses and the instructors' contracts at little or no cost to the college. Since part-timers are not provided security of employment or tenure, the colleges can hire or fire part-time faculty as a means of responding to sudden shifts in student interests, enrollments, and state allotted funds for community college education.

The third premise for hiring part- rather than full-time faculty is that the instruction provided by part-timers is assumed to be of equal quality to that provided by the regular staff. Among the arguments advanced in support of this assumption are the following: since part-timers hold the same teaching credentials as full-timers, the instruction delivered should be the same, and both groups perform the same instructional activities — they meet their classes, give their lectures, listen to student presentations, and turn in the grades. To date, few if any studies have been conducted to determine whether, in general, students who enroll in courses taught by adjunct faculty receive instruction inferior to that offered by full-time instructors.

The Study

The purpose of this chapter is to examine the assumption that the instruction provided by part-time faculty is similar to that of full-time faculty. In order to test the accuracy of this premise, comparisons will be made between part-time and full-time faculty in eleven areas that are likely to affect the quality of instruction. The criteria used to compare the part-time to the full-time faculty are teaching experience, degree attainment, length of time teaching at the current institution, participation in the selection of course materials, reading requirements, use of instructional media, use of instructional support services, use of out-of-class activities for course, grading practices, instructor availability to students, and involvement in instructional and professional development activities.

These comparisons can be made using data obtained from the following sources: a nationwide survey of background characteristics, work-related values, attitudes and behaviors of representative samples of 378 part-time and 1,603 full-time two-year college humanities instructors and nonhumanities chairpersons (Cohen and Brawer, 1977); two nationwide studies of the instructional practices used by representative samples of 351 part-time and 1,669 full-time humanities, science, and social science faculty members in a predesignated course they were currently teaching (Cohen, 1977; Cohen and Hill, 1978); and research studies that compared part- and full-time instructors in the two-year college on factors related to instruction. The three nationwide surveys were conducted by the Center for the Study of Community Colleges (CSCC) under grants from the National Endowment for the Humanities and the National Science Foundation. Unless noted otherwise, the results presented in the remainder of this chapter are based on the three national studies conducted by the CSCC in 1975, 1977, and 1978.

Teaching Experience. The findings of the instructor surveys showed that the full-time faculty staff had much more teaching experience than the part-time staff. Close to 90 percent of the former as compared to 55 percent of the latter had three or more years of teaching experience. The difference between the two groups was even more dramatic at the lower end of the teaching experience scale where 4 percent of the full-time faculty members had less than one year of teaching experience as compared to 18 percent of the part-time faculty members. Similar findings have also been reported in other studies of two-year college faculty (Kennedy, 1967; Lombardi, 1975).

Continuity of Employment. Part-timers were not only less experienced in teaching than full-timers, but they had taught fewer years in their current institution. Data from the 1975 CSCC faculty survey showed that 55 percent of the part-time instructors had taught at their current college for two years or less whereas only 13 percent of the full-timers fell into that category.

Teaching experience and length of time at one college are likely to enhance a community college instructor's ability to conduct a course in that it takes time for faculty to learn what instructional support services are available (library assistance, learning resource center), what each service has to offer (types of media materials available), and what procedures must be followed to gain access to such services (ordering class textbooks and supplies); it takes time for faculty to develop their courses and to devise effective instructional techniques to reach the types of students who enroll in the classes they teach; and it takes time for faculty to become sufficiently conversant with institutional policies and requirements to provide their students with sound advice concerning the curriculum. The difficulties new part-time faculty have in learning about their instructional environment are compounded by the findings that most community colleges do not provide formal orientation and in-service training programs for their part-time teachers (Bender and Breuder, 1973; Cooke and Hurlburt, 1976; Lombardi, 1975; Moe, 1977; Persinger, 1977; Sewell, 1976).

Degree Attainment. It is generally assumed that the more graduate work faculty members have had, the better qualified they are to teach at the college level. The findings of the instructor surveys revealed that 21 percent of the part-timers as compared to 5 percent of the full-timers had not earned an academic degree beyond the baccalaureate.

Selection of Course Materials. Respondents to the instructor surveys were asked to indicate the extent to which they had control over the selection of reading materials to be used in their course. A much greater percentage of part-time than full-time faculty indicated that they had no say in the selection of such materials used in their class (textbooks, 53 percent versus 11 percent; laboratory materials and workbooks, 50 percent versus 9 percent); and collections of readings 12 percent versus 5 percent). It seems safe to assume that many faculty members would find it easier to teach a course based on materials of their own choice than on those selected by others. Some support for this assertion comes from the finding that 20 percent of the part-time faculty and 8 percent of the full-time faculty said that their course could be improved if they had more freedom to choose course materials. Some part-time faculty members may also face constraints with other aspects of their course since they have little or no participation in departmental decisions concerning course content and curriculum development (Cooke and Hurlburt, 1976; Guichard, Mangham, and Gallery, 1975).

Reading Requirements for Students. One of the questions asked of the two-year college faculty members was "How many pages do you require your students to read in textbooks, laboratory manuals, collections of readings, reference books, magazines and journals, and newspapers?" (CSCC, 1978, 1979). On average, part-timers required their students to read 402 pages for a course; full-timers, 551 pages. These figures on the number of pages seem somewhat inflated. Inspection of the survey forms showed that many of the respondents in both instructor groups counted all the pages in their textbooks as required reading.

Use of Instructional Media. A much greater percentage of full-time than part-time faculty reported that they used some form of instructional media in their classes (45 percent versus 33 percent). The instructors were also asked to indicate which of fourteen types of instructional aids they used in their courses. With one exception (three-dimensional models), a higher percentage of full-time than part-time faculty used the various instructional media considered. To illustrate, full-timers were more likely than the part-timers to use films (60 percent versus 46 percent), overhead projected transparencies (45 percent versus 30 percent), scientific instruments (42 percent versus 28 percent), slides (39 percent versus 30 percent), filmstrips (29 percent versus 19 percent), and video tapes (26 percent versus 15 percent). One reason for these differences is apparent: A much greater percentage of the part-time than full-time faculty members (43 percent versus 32 percent) said they did not have access to media production facilities and/or assistance.

Three additional factors (noted in other studies) which would serve to discourage part-time faculty from using instructional media are: (1) lack of awareness of what resources are available; (2) lack of familiarity with procedures on how to acquire desired materials; and (3) lack of sufficient lead time (resulting from last-minute hiring) to obtain materials which need to be ordered in advance (Seitz, 1971). That the community college instructors viewed media as a valuable instructional resource is evidenced in the finding that close to 40 percent of the faculty stated that they could make their course more effective if they had access to more media and/or instructional materials.

Use of Out-of-Class Activities. The full-timers were more likely than the part-timers either to recommend or require that their students attend each of eleven out-of-class events on the campus or in the community. The largest difference between the two groups was in the percentage who encouraged their students to attend on-campus educational films (42 percent versus 30 percent), other films (36 percent versus 30 percent), outside lectures (44 percent versus 34 percent), television programs (48 percent versus 41 percent), theatrical productions (45 percent versus 33 percent), and concerts or recitals (38 percent versus 31 percent). (The latter two items were asked of only the humanities faculty.) An insight into these differences comes from the findings of the 1975 CSCC instructor survey which showed that the part-timers were more than three times as likely as the full-timers to respond "Don't Know" to the question of whether the college provided students with too few, sufficient, or too many colloquiums and seminars (26 percent versus 7 percent), lectures (20 percent versus 4 percent), exhibits (19 percent versus 5 percent), concerts and recitals (19 percent versus 4 percent), and films (18 percent versus 5 percent). It is not surprising that part-time humanities faculty being less aware of humanities-related activities at their college would less frequently recommend them to their students.

Use of Instructional Support Services. Most educational institutions provide their faculty with support services designed to enhance the instructional process. Respondents to the surveys were asked to indicate whether each of eight college support services were available to them, and if so, whether or not they took advantage of them in the particular class used in the survey. Responses showed that full-timers were more likely than the part-timers to use clerical help (68 percent versus 51 percent), library and bibliographic assistance (43 percent versus 34 percent), media production facilities or assistance (40 percent versus 31 percent), tutors (32 percent versus 22 percent), and test-serving facilities (24 percent versus 13 percent). Less than 12 percent of the faculty in each group used the other two services (considered-readers and instructional assistants).

Not only were the part-timers less likely than the full-timers to use most of the support services, they were also less likely to report that the various services were available to them. These results are consistent with those reported by Cooke and Hurlburt (1976) who noted that the part-timers were asked to work under less favorable conditions than their full-time conterparts.

Grading Practices. A greater percentage of full-time than part-time faculty based their grades on student activities which, in most instances, required out-of-class time to grade. These activities included quick score objective tests (73 percent versus 64 percent), essay exams (61 percent versus 53 percent), field reports (13 percent versus 11 percent), and workbook completion (16 percent versus 11 percent). Conversely, a greater percentage of part-timers than full-timers based their grades on student activities that could be graded in class. These included oral reports (30 percent versus 26 percent), participation in class discussions (55 percent versus 46 percent), and regular class attendance (51 percent versus 41 percent). There were no differences in the percentage of part-time and full-time instructors who based their grades in part on papers written out of class (45 percent) and on papers written in class (20 percent).

Availability to Students. Up to this point, comparisons between the instructional practices of part-time and full-time faculty have centered on the classroom. However, effective instruction also involves contact with students outside the classroom in such areas as curriculum and career counseling, tutoring, individual consultation, and informal exchanges of ideas and information. Along these lines Wilson and others (1975) studied undergraduate teaching and found that the effective instructor "more frequently interacts with students beyond the classroom . . . , discussing careers and educational plans, course-related ideas, campus issues, and problems of immediate personal concern to individual students" (p. 192). The value of student-faculty interactions on student development has been demonstrated in studies of college students (Centra and Rock, 1971) and in theories relating the level of student-faculty involvement outside the classroom to college persistence (Pascarella and Terezini, 1977; Spady, 1970; Tinto, 1975).

Instructional practices found in many two-year colleges — such as the lack of office space for part-time instructors to meet with students (Bender and Breuder, 1973; Sewell and others, 1976) and failure, on the part of many college administrators, to provide part-time instructors with adequate opportunities and incentives to increase their understanding of the college or to meet with students outside of class — serve to discourage part-timers from adequately fulfilling the extra-instructional responsibilities that they owe to their students.

Involvement in Professional Activities. In terms of involvement in professional growth activities, a higher percentage of the full-time than part-time faculty who responded to the 1975 Center for the Study of Community Colleges (CSCC) instructor survey reported that they read scholarly journals (77 percent versus 67 percent) or professional education journals (39 percent versus 26 percent), belonged to a professional organization (82 percent versus 63 percent), attended a professional meeting (48 percent versus 38 percent), or presented a professional paper (11 percent versus 8 percent). Additional information concerning involvement in professional development activities — including interaction with colleagues — was obtained from a series of items on the CSCC 1977 and 1978 instructor surveys which asked faculty to indicate what was needed to make their courses better. A much higher percentage of part-time than full-time instructors noted that their course could be improved through greater interaction with colleagues and administrators (29 percent versus 17 percent). The full-timers, however, were more interested in release time to develop their courses and/or materials (41 percent versus 20 percent), and in participation in professional development programs (30 percent versus 23 percent). These results are consistent with the literature on part-time instructors which indicates that many of them have no more than slight contact with their peers (Marsh and Lamb, 1975), and relatively few attend professional development activities when given the opportunity to do so (Cooke and Hurlburt, 1976; Marsh and Lamb, 1975; Moe, 1977).

Summary of Results

The primary purpose of this study was to test the assumption that the instruction-related activites of part-time faculty were similar to those of full-time faculty. The findings reported in this chapter demonstrate that the part-timers differed from the full-timers on most of the measures related to instructional practices. Specifically, when compared to their full-time counterparts, part-time instructors were found to have less teaching experience, to have taught fewer years at their current institution, and to hold lower academic credentials. The adjunct instructor also differed from the full-timer in that he had less choice in the selection of materials to be used in his course, assigned fewer pages to read, used less instructional media, recommended or required students to attend fewer out-of-class activities, and placed less emphasis on written assignments in determining student grades. In addition, part-timers were less aware of campus activities and events, were less likely to have access to or to use instructional support services, were less likely to have out-of-class contacts with student, colleagues, or administrators, and were likely to have less determination in such matters as departmental affairs, course content, curriculum development, and textbook selection. In terms of professional development activities, part-timers differed from full-timers in that they read fewer scholarly and educational journals, were less likely to hold memberships in professional associations or to attend or participate in professional meetings, and were less likely to express a desire for release time to develop their course or to participate in professional growth programs. Perhaps because of this, they were more likely than the full-timers to express the need for more interaction with colleagues and administrators. These findings clearly demonstrate that there are differences in the instruction-related practices of part-time and full-time faculty.

Quality of Instruction

The question that now needs to be addressed is whether the current practice of employing part-time instead of full-time faculty detracts from the overall quality of the two-year colleges' educational programs. If, as it is commonly assumed, certain factors (academic degree attainment, teaching experience, continuity of employment, knowledge of one's educational environment, use of instructional technologies, involvement in educational policy decisions, maintenance of office hours, interaction with colleagues, and participation in professional development activites) contribute to program effectiveness, then one could conclude that the quality of instruction provided by a college is likely to be adversely affected as the proportion of part-time to full-time faculty increases.

Conclusion

The employment policy of community colleges should be designed to maximize the quality of instruction provided by the institutions. Given this objective, the decision to hire part-time instead of full-time instructors could be justified if the colleges, students, regular staff, programs, and the institutions themselves would benefit. Unless this objective is met, the educational wisdom of substituting part-time faculty members for full-time faculty members would seem difficult to defend. The challenge facing two-year college educators is to develop sound programs (recruitment, orientation, development, evaluation) and policies (support services to part-timers, compensation for out-of-class activities such as office hours and participation in faculty development activities) that will enable part-time faculty to provide the same quality of instruction to students as members of the full-time staff are able to offer.

References

American Association of Community and Junior Colleges. *1979 Community, Junior, and Technical College Directory.* Washington, D.C.: American Association of Community and Junior Colleges, 1979.

Bender, L. W., and Breuder, R. L. "Part-Time Teachers—'Step-Children' of the Community College." *Community College Review,* 1973, *1* (1), 29–37.

36

Center for the Study of Community Colleges, *Humanities Instruction Survey*. Los Angeles, Calif.: Center for the Study of Community Colleges, 1978.

Center for the Study of Community Colleges, *Science Instruction Survey*. Los Angeles, Calif.: Center for the Study of Community Colleges, 1979.

Centra, J., and Rock, D. "College Environments and Student Achievement." *American Educational Research Journal*, 1971, *8*, 623–634.

Cohen, A. M. *Instructional Practices in the Humanities*. Los Angeles, Calif.: Center for the Study of Community Colleges, 1977. (ED 160 145)

Cohen, A. M., and Brawer, F. B. *The Two-Year College Instructor Today*. New York: Praeger, 1977.

Cohen, A. M., and Hill, A. *Instructional Practices in the Sciences*. Los Angeles, Calif.: Center for the Study of Community Colleges, 1978. (ED 160 144)

Cooke, J. L., and Hurlburt, A. S. "Part-Time Faculty Needs Full-Time Support." *Community College Review*, 1976, *4* (1), 15–18.

Guichard, G., Mangham, C., and Gallery, G. M. *Part-Time Employment, Item 8*. Sacramento: California Community Colleges Office of the Chancellor, 1975. (ED 111 464)

Kennedy, G. "Preparation, Orientation, Utilization and Acceptance of Part-Time Instructors." *Junior College Journal*, 1967, *37* (7), 14–15.

Lombardi, J. *Part-Time Faculty in Community Colleges*. Topical Paper No. 54. Los Angeles: Calif.: ERIC Clearinghouse for Junior Colleges, 1975. (ED 115 316)

Marsh, J. P., and Lamb, T. (Eds.). An Introduction to the Part-Time Teaching Situation with Particular Emphasis on its Impact at Napa Community College. Unpublished paper, 1975. (ED 125 683, available in microfiche only.)

Moe, J. "A Staff Development Model for Part-Time Instructors." In T. O'Banion (Ed.), *New Directions for Community Colleges: Developing Staff Potential*. no. 19. San Francisco: Jossey-Bass, 1977.

Pascarella, E., and Terenzini, P. "Informal Interaction with Faculty and Freshman Ratings of the Academic and Non-Academic Experience of College." *Journal of Educational Research*, 1976, *70*, 35–41.

Pascarella, E., and Terenzini, P. "Patterns of Student-Faculty Informal Interaction Beyond the Classroom and Voluntary Freshman Attrition." *Journal of Higher Education*, 1977, *48* (5), 541–552.

Persinger, G. R. *Professional Development for Part-Time Faculty*. Research and Demonstration Project. Wheeling, Va.: Council for North Central Community and Junior Colleges, 1977. (ED 168 664)

Seitz, J. E. "Professional Orientations and Attitudes of Part-Time Junior College Faculty". Unpublished doctoral dissertation, Southern Illinois University, 1971.

Sewell, D. H., and others. *Report on a Statewide Survey About Part-Time Faculty in California Community Colleges*. Sacramento: California Community and Junior College Association, 1976. (ED 118 195)

Spady, W. "Dropouts from Higher Education: An Interdisciplinary Review and Synthesis." *Interchange*, 1970, *1*, 64–85.

Tinto, V. "Dropout from Higher Education: A Theoretical Synthesis of Recent Research." *Review of Educational Research*, 1975, *45*, 89–125.

Wilson, R. J., and others. *College Professors and Their Impact on Students*. New York: Wiley, 1975.

Jack Friedlander is a research associate at the Center for the Study of Community Colleges and a staff writer at the ERIC Clearinghouse for Junior Colleges. He has published several articles on part-time faculty.

When part-time instructors outnumber full-time faculty,
a community college must provide an adjunct faculty
development program.

Burlington County College: Development Program for Adjunct Faculty

Harmon B. Pierce
Rosemary T. Miller

Burlington County College (BCC) is a public two-year comprehensive community college located in suburban-rural central New Jersey, some thirty miles east of Philadelphia. The college opened in fall 1969 and presently enrolls about 6,200 full- and part-time students (4,300 FTE) on its permanent campus and several satellite locations. One of the satellite locations is a 7,000-square foot, leased facility located in a large shopping center. The full-time faculty (1977–80) numbers 110, and adjunct faculty fluctuates according to semester but may exceed 170 in the fall.

While the purpose of the chapter is to give a background description of the BCC staff development program for adjunct faculty, the remarks immediately following serve to provide a context within which the reader may view this segment of the overall faculty development plan.

Most new community college instructors approach teaching with rather traditional concepts of higher education and their role in it. The community college usually must give them an awareness of the mission of the institution and a productive attitude toward it. Moreover, these teachers must learn how to serve the heterogeneous student population they will encounter in the comprehensive community college. Colleges are obligated by law in some states and collective bagaining agreements in others to provide a staff development plan to complement and strengthen performance evaluation policies. The most important reason for the existence of faculty development plans, however, is the improvement of student learning.

With this in mind, BCC has developed a plan for faculty development entailing pre- and inservice training, support personnel, financial incentives, and professional growth activities. The basic elements of the program are outlined below:

1.0 Organized Training Activities
    1.1 Preservice Training for Full-Time Faculty
    1.2 Inservice Training for Full-Time Faculty
    1.3 Inservice Training for Adjunct Faculty

2.0 Support for Education, Travel, and Other Professionally Enriching Activities
    2.1 Tuition Payment for Graduate Work
    2.2 Long-Term Leave
    2.3 Short-Term Leave
    2.4 Sabbatical Leave
    2.5 Exchange Teaching Leave
    2.6 Faculty Travel

3.0 Incentives for Faculty Development of Instructional Materials
    3.1 Faculty Fellowships
    3.2 Released Time
    3.3 Copyright Policy
    3.4 Educational Materials Sales Office

4.0 Instructional Development Center
    4.1 Director of Educational Development
    4.1.1 Educational Development Team

5.0 Professional Library Collection

6.0 Division of Learning Resources
    6.1 The Library
    6.2 Reference Libraries
    6.3 Coordinator of Media Services (CMS)
    6.3.1 Graphic Arts
    6.3.2 Photography
    6.3.3 Print Shop
    6.3.4 Audio Production
    6.3.5 Video Production
    6.4 Instructional Programmer/Bibliographer

7.0 Other Personnel Supporting Faculty Development Efforts
    7.1 Director of Instructional Computer Service
    7.2 Director of Institutional Research and Planning
    7.3 Instructional Assistant (IA)
    7.4 Technical and Clerical Support Personnel

Program Structure, Management, Policies, and Personnel

New Full-Time Faculty. All new full-time faculty are given a concentrated preservice training program to acquaint them with the college's philosophy and the instructional techniques they will be expected to adopt. In the ten years since the college opened, there have been ten preservice training institutes. The first session for the charter faculty was conducted during the summer of 1969. The session was seven weeks long and was designed to give the faculty preliminary training in writing objectives and using different instructional strategies and, also, to allow them time to do the initial instructional development work to start fall classes.

This original institute was designed and conducted by the dean of instruction with the assistance of several outside specialists. It subsequently became evident that the college needed its own full-time specialist knowledgeable in the fields of instructional development and educational technology if staff training and development were to receive adequate emphasis. The position of education development officer (EDO) was created, and the staff development and training functions centered in this office. The EDO and the educational development team have evolved into the unified organization described later in this chapter.

The second preservice training session, the first to be designed by the EDO, was held in August 1970 prior to the opening of the fall semester. This session was reduced to three weeks, reflecting greater efficiency in the organization of the training. The second workshop was federally funded under the Educational Professions Development Act.

The third preservice training session was held during August 1971. Through additional staff experience, the workshop was reduced to two weeks and made extensive use of the kinds of materials used in the 1970 workshop. Two-week sessions scheduled during August were the format used for training new full-time faculty from 1971 to 1975. Participants were paid on the regular summer teaching salary scale and attendance was required.

During the fall, 1976 institute, the training sessions were moved from August to September and integrated into the academic schedules of new faculty. Instructional materials were revised and more independent study packets were coordinated with scheduled training sessions and individual consultation with staff developers.

Adjunct Faculty. Burlington County College annually employs some 170 adjunct faculty members in a variety of disciplines. Student and division evaluations of part-time staff members indicated that training was needed in such areas as the nature and mission of the comprehensive community college, its teaching methods, and the improvement of instruction. Adjuncts also needed to become more familiar with BCC, its students, and the programs and services it offered.

During the 1971 through 1979 academic years, inservice institutes for part-time faculty were held each fall and winter semesters. Designed and led by the EDO, and utilizing senior full-time faculty as helping instructors, each institute consisted of five, three-hour sessions held on sequential Saturday mornings. The syllabus for these sessions was modified and shortened from the preservice institutes and stressed more immediate need and short-term development activities as well as orientation to the college.

Over 85 percent of the present adjunct faculty has now completed one of these institutes. Participants are paid seventy-five dollars if they complete the work assigned and attend all sessions. Completion of the institute also is one of the requisites for advancement to senior adjunct faculty status and higher pay. However, the greatest incentive appears to come from those who have attended previous sessions and recommend the program as having been helpful to them.

As in the case with the preservice institute for full-time faculty, the format for the adjunct institute has been integrated with appropriate materials from the preservice training program. New adjuncts are given a training syllabus and a one-day briefing during the first week of classes. This session consists of a general orientation to the college and is based on the adjunct faculty handbook.

Administrative Organization. Faculty development activities at BCC are administratively organized as follows: The president of the college has reporting to him a vice-president for academic and student affairs (VPASA). Reporting to the VPASA is the dean of academic affairs, who has responsibility for all instructional divisions, learning resources and educational and staff development activities. The director of educational development reports to the dean. This person provides overall supervision of the faculty development program and, through the dean, coordinates this effort with the instructional division heads and faculty.

From two to five experienced faculty may be released up to one fourth time to work with the development specialist to form an educational development team. This concept was implemented four years ago and has been a successful developmental tool. It was apparent from the beginning that faculty react more favorably to advice from experienced colleagues than from full-time developers brought in from outside, however occasional outside consultants are helpful. (It should be noted that the staff developer is not directly involved in administrative evaluation of faculty performance. The developer will provide assessments of instruction to a division chairperson only if the faculty member being evaluated requests it.)

Program Design

The following discussion of "Program Design" is from the faculty training manual prepared by the Office of Educational Development. Training activities are designed by the development team and implemented with help from appropriate faculty and administrators.

Because the preservice training institute and the adjunct training institute at BCC have been designed to accomodate new as well as adjunct staff members, the educational development team has isolated the competencies most needed by a beginning staff member. They are as follows: A staff member at BCC must be familiar with the campus physical plant, the counseling services, and the institutional philosophy. He must be conversant with the role of the community college in higher education and the specific characteristics of community college students, particularly those attennding BCC. He must be able to design a course syllabus, a learning packet, evaluate a course and student performance, operate learning equipment, and understand the role of the instructional assistant at BCC. An adjunct faculty member must be able to interpret a course syllabus and learning packet as designed by a full-time faculty member.

New learning packets and many new audio/visual learning materials were side benefits of the training institutes. Current learning packets are closely coordinated to required competencies. (See Figure 1 for detail of the packets.)

Figure 1. Adjunct Training Institute

I. **Course Description**
   The purpose of the adjunct training institute is to prepare faculty members to make decisions about methods of instruction and evaluation; develop skills in the design of syllabi, packets, unit tests, and course evaluation; and to become familiar with the philosophy of the college and its students.

II. **Prerequisites**
   Employment at BCC as an adjunct faculty member.

III. **Rationale**
   This course is designed for adjunct faculty to provide them with the skills to design and present quality learning experiences in accord with the college's systems approach to instruction. By completing the course activities, the faculty member should be better prepared to meet the special needs of the BCC student.

IV. **General Course Goals**
   A. *Knowledge/Skills*
      1. The faculty member will be able to recognize and design course syllabi, packets, tests, units, and feedback devices.
      2. The faculty member will learn what is expected of a faculty member at BCC.
      3. The faculty member will be able to use the instructional equipment and services available at BCC.
   B. *Attitude*
      1. The faculty member will form a positive attitude toward the use of the systems approach to learning.
      2. The faculty member will develop a reasonable policy for attendance, grading, and testing.

V. **Instructional Modes**
   Large Group
   Small Group
   Independent Study

VI. **Descriptions of Instructional Units**
   The Community College Student — SER 104
   This unit is a slide/tape presentation designed to acquaint the adjunct faculty member with the community college student generally and the characteristics and problems specific to the student at BCC.

   The College Tour — SER 102
   This includes a booklet designed to orient the adjunct faculty member to the physical plant and provide a ready reference to campus locations.

Institutional Philosophy — SER 101
This slide — tape presentation briefly explains the systems approach to education as it relates to the institutional philosophy at BCC.

The Course Syllabus — SER 105
A printed packet describes preparation of a course syllabus.

The Role of the Community College in Higher Education — SER 103
This videotape presentation defines the role of the community college in higher education generally and, more specifically, the role of BCC in the community.

Institutional Facilities and Services — SER 109
A booklet explains the operation of various kinds of instruction equipment and educational services which the college provides.

The Learning Packet — SER 106
This unit is itself a learning packet which covers the objectives, pretests, learning activities, posttests, and course revision data. It also includes a section that allows the user to write a sample learning packet and review samples of packets used by other faculty members.

The Evaluation of Students — SER 107
An audio-tutorial slide/tape presentation covers test construction, item analysis, and other evaluation tools used by the faculty at BCC.

Course Evaluation — SER 108
An audio-tutorial slide tape presents evaluation and its effects on course revision.
VII. **Evaluation of the Adjunct Faculty Institute Participants**
A. Completion of all units.
B. Submission of all assignments to the Office of Educational Development.
VIII. **Program Resources**
With the exception of the 1970 preservice institute, all staff development activities from 1969 through August 1979 were completely supported by the college. The annual cost of all development personnel and activities varies but ranges between $50,000 and $120,000, depending on funds available. The adjunct faculty segment usually costs about $4,500 per year.
IX. **Program Evaluation**
Adjunct faculty participants complete written evaluations of formal training sessions and learning materials. As the year progresses, revision suggestions are solicited by the development team and are considered in preparing materials for the coming year. Adjunct faculty rank the inservice institutes high with regard to accomplishment of their objectives, and follow-up surveys indicate participants gained knowledge and desired attitudes. Most importantly, student ratings of institute graduates invariably improve, indicating that the experience is effective in changing faculty behavior and in producing better instruction.
X. **The Future of the Program**
BCC is pleased with the adjunct faculty institutes as they are presently conducted and plans no drastic revisions. The program will continue indefinitely.

In an attempt to make these learning materials more usable, the packets were designed to accommodate both group and independent study. In this way, persons who are employed after the formal preservice activities have been concluded will be able to receive the information at any time of the year. Furthermore, many of these learning activities are appropriate for professional staff members who do not have faculty rank.

In September 1976, four syllabi were constructed for the use of staff members. Although many of the units were included in all syllabi, all staff members did not need to acquire all the competencies. (For example, there is no need for an instructional assistant to learn to construct a learning packet. However, an instructional assistant certainly must know how to interpret a learning packet for a student.) The syllabi reflect varying requirements.

Figure 1 has a syllabus and descriptions of learning packets. Required learning materials are housed in the math lab except for a videotape on the role of the community college in higher education kept in presentation services. Reserve reading materials are on hand in the library.

These learning experiences are presented in various ways. *Terms and Conditions of Employment* and *The Role of the Community College in Higher Education* are large group activities; viewers for the *Role* videotape are split into small groups for discussion, and *The College Tour* combines selected faculty and new people.

Several of the units are workshops scheduled for the first semester. They are *Institutional Facilities and Services, The Learning Packet, The Course Syllabus, The Evaluation of Students,* and *The Evaluation of a Course.* The remaining packets are independent study, but members of the educational development team are available for assistance.

The adjunct training institute usually is scheduled five Saturdays during the fall semester. Although many of the competencies required for adjunct and full-time faculty are the same, because they are not on campus as frequently as full-time staff, adjunct needs are often somewhat different. For this reason, all units required for adjunct training are scheduled as formal sessions. This does not preclude adjunct faculty use of the packets in independent study, however, all assignments must be handed in if this method is elected.

A typical (9:00 A.M.–12:00 P.M. Saturday) adjunct training institute schedule is as follows:

October 2	*The Role of the Community College* and *The College Tour*
October 16	*Institutional Facilities and Services*
October 29	*The Learning Packet*
November 11	*Evaluation of Students* and *Course Evaluation*
December 3	*The Course Syllabus*

Harmon B. Pierce is president of Burlington County College, in Pemberton, New Jersey. He also has served the institution as vice-president for academic and student affairs and, prior to that, as dean of instruction.

Rosemary T. Miller currently holds the rank of associate professor at Burlington County College. She has served as faculty associate for staff development and professional development specialist at that institution. After having served for two years as Northeast regional representative for the National Council for Staff, Program and Organizational Development, Miller is now treasurer for the organization.

*One model to develop part-time faculty potential uses six
components. The design addresses the needs of small
institutions with limited resources.*

Realizing Part-Time
Faculty Potential

Michael H. Parsons

There are new faces on the campuses of America's two-year colleges.
Senior citizens, part-time students, and women returning to school
after raising families make up large segments of the student body.
Increasingly these new students are being taught by part-time faculty.
More than half the teachers in two-year colleges in 1978 were part-time
(Gleazer, 1979). The trend toward the increased use of part-time faculty has caused concern in community college circles. Haddad and
Dickens conducted a needs-assessment with thirty-five two-year colleges that are participating in the ACCTion Consortium for professional development. "Part-time faculty development was the top concern" (1978, p. 22). The need to integrate part-time teachers into the
instructional design of the two-year college is critical if their potential is
to be realized.

Two recent national surveys highlight the assistance needed by
part-time faculty. Friedlander (1979) analyzed data drawn from the
Center for the Study of Community Colleges' surveys of humanities
and science teachers. He indicated that part-time teachers have less
teaching experience, use less media to support instruction, require less

reading of their students, and are less involved in educationally related activities than are their full-time colleagues. Obviously part-time teachers are not as well versed as full-time ones in the process of instruction. They are hired for their subject matter expertise. Therefore, a model is needed to assist them in presenting their knowledge to the student.

Hagerstown Junior College (HJC) is located in Washington County, Maryland. The college mirrors the national trend; 49 percent of its faculty are full time and 51 percent are part time. For the past six years the college has been developing a model to ensure that parity exists between the instruction provided by full-time and part-time faculty.

Faculty Development Model

The model consists of six components. They are recruitment, orientation, communication, support services, an instructional clinic, and evaluation. Each of the components addresses a need identified by part-time faculty in a survey conducted to determine how the college could assist them in becoming more effective teachers (Annual Survey of Part-Time Faculty Services, 1977). Because the components are mutually reinforcing, all dimensions of a need are given attention. The model is also self-correcting. As needs change, components are modified. The model is worthy of examination.

Recruitment. Often the new student takes a single course; for him, that teacher personifies instruction at the college. Course listings at HJC do not indicate whether the teacher is full-time or part time, yet students have the right to expect a single standard of quality. Therefore, the college must locate an individual who possesses the needed expertise and has the potential for delivering it.

HJC uses a search committee to locate part-time faculty candidates. The committee draws upon a variety of sources: program advisory committees, the local secondary school system, and local businesses and industries. Full-time faculty are encouraged to recommend candidates. If no acceptable individual emerges, newspaper advertisement is used. The committee, in cooperation with the appropriate division head at the college, screens the applicants and recommends its choice to the dean of instruction. The procedure has resulted in a nucleus of qualified part-time teachers. Without a procedure a college relies on chance. The result, too often, is a mediocre instructor and a dissatisfied student.

Orientation. The orientation process at HJC begins with the employment interview. To open a communications link the division head in whose area the part-time faculty member will teach is present and provides text materials, course syllabus, and sample examinations. He also introduces part-time instructors to full-time instructors who are teaching the same, or related, courses. The merits of a "buddy system" are stressed, and the part-time instructor is encouraged to contact the division head if any problems arise. The goal of the initial interview is to establish a progressing relationship.

Since many part-time faculty are unfamiliar with the college campus, a tour is provided. Included is the appropriate classroom or laboratory, library, bookstore, and cafeteria. If the part-time instructor is to be of service to the students, he must know his way around campus.

Meetings cannot identify all needs of a part-time teacher. Therefore, HJC developed a part-time faculty handbook. The publication answers the questions about instruction most frequently asked by part-time personnel. It lowers anxiety, replaces repetitive briefings, and provides a ready reference for unanticipated questions. Part-time faculty members are urged to read the handbook prior to beginning their teaching assignment.

The first step in the orientation process is the part-time-faculty workshop. There are several objectives. First, other people the part-time faculty member is likely to work with are introduced and their functions are explained. Second, part-time personnel are given identification cards and parking stickers. Third, any questions regarding the part-time handbook are solicited and answered. This exchange has proven useful to both full- and part-time personnel. Finally, the division heads assemble their part-time faculty to discuss topical matters. The workshop is designed to be the first step in giving the part-time faculty member a share in the college that will grow throughout the association.

Communications. With the onset of teaching responsibility, a new phase of the development model begins. Part-time faculty are busy people; maximum benefit must be derived from limited contact. Failure to maintain contact will undermine previous efforts. HJC has adopted a series of activities intended to reinforce the orientation process with a minimal investment of time, effort, and resources.

Because many of the part-time faculty teach in the evening, HJC has established an evening duty calendar. Each of the college's administrators and counselors is on duty several times each semester.

The evening calendar is given to each part-time faculty member. There are several reasons for so doing. Part-time faculty are made aware that they may refer questions or students to a knowledgeable person. Also, if a problem arises, there is someone to contact. It also makes it easier for the part-time instructor to meet with a specific administrator or counselor.

The process takes advantage of mail and college announcements. HJC has a selective mailing procedure for part-time faculty — those who teach at an extension center receive mail at home. Each part-time instructor receives the weekly bulletin which contains announcements of general interest to the college community. Part-time faculty are encouraged to notify students of the contents and to submit announcements. The purpose of this process is to reinforce the communications responsibility of all faculty — full- and part-time — and to underscore the importance of part-time instructors to the college community. When there are announcements of special events of interest to part-time faculty, these are included in the selective mailing. Every attempt is made to ensure that part-time faculty feel a sense of identity with HJC. As Smith indicates, "critical commitment which a college must make to the adjunct faculty is to . . . communicate the duties of adjunct teachers to them" (1977, p. 36).

Support Services. To deliver equivalent instruction, part-time faculty require the same instructional support systems as full-time. Therefore, HJC offers the following services. First, the college's media center works closely with them. Equipment, funds for audio-visual material rental, and personnel are available to part-time teachers. Second, the college supports its instructional programs with a series of individualized learning centers. All teachers may refer their students to the centers, integrate center services into the instructional process, or work with center personnel to develop alternate approaches to course objectives. Finally, the college makes clerical assistance, office space, and instructional materials readily available to part-time personnel. The process includes the division head, evening coordinator, and clerical services center. Though the benefit seems obvious, there are two reasons for this. Ease of access to services and materials frees the part-time teachers from concern for trivia and allows them to concentrate on quality instruction. Equally, the services are a tangible indication of the college's regard for part-time faculty: they result in a sense of identification with the college's mission by the part-time teacher.

Instructional Clinic. To ensure faculty development continues at the college, in 1976, an instructional clinic was established to allow college faculty and staff to address problems that emanate from the teaching-learning process (Parsons, 1976). From the beginning, part-time faculty have been notified of the meetings and encouraged to participate. In one instance, a part-time teacher chaired a session. Since 1978 special sessions have been conducted to foster instructional development techniques among part-time faculty. Topics including performance objectives, effective lecture technique, increased student motivation, and diagnosis of teaching-learning problems have been discussed (Parsons, 1979). The college received a mini-grant from the Maryland Division of Vocational-Technical Education to provide stipends for part-time teachers participating in the clinic. Again a parity of instruction is the purpose of expanding the clinic to part-time faculty.

Evaluation. If the model described above appears to be disjointed, the final phase, evaluation, is designed to integrate the components into a functional whole. The college uses a two-way evaluation procedure: The part-time faculty member's teaching is evaluated and the part-time teacher evaluates the services received from HJC. Results of both evaluations are assessed and used to improve recruitment, orientation, communication, support services, and the instructional clinic. The process of continuous evaluation and modification keeps the HJC model relevant to an ever-changing environment.

Each part-time teacher is evaluated by students and supervisors during the first course taught and annually thereafter. After evaluation, the part-time teacher and the division head confer. Goals for instructional improvement are agreed upon and recorded. This evaluation procedure has improved instruction and increased student satisfaction.

The teachers also have a say. Part-time faculty are surveyed to determine the utility of the procedures, people, and support systems provided by HJC (Annual Survey of Part-Time Faculty Services, 1977). The results of the annual survey are used to improve the development model. The instructional clinic, evening counseling hours, and several changes in the part-time faculty handbook have emerged from the survey. In essence the synergistic nature of the evaluation process has allowed the college to balance services to part-time faculty and instructional improvement in a single, thriving system.

Future Directions

The HJC approach to the challenge presented by part-time faculty is dynamic. As the needs of the participants and the directions of the college change, modifications are made. Three areas under investigation merit discussion.

First, the college is considering the formation of a part-time faculty advisory committee composed of teachers from the part-time faculty. They will assist with communication, recruitment, and orientation while helping to validate the evaluation of services rendered to part-time faculty.

Second, HJC is exploring the use of a "buddy system" wherein a full-time or senior part-time teacher will be assigned to each new part-time instructor. This is expected to make certain that the orientation process is effective and to reduce the sense of isolation experienced by new part-time teachers.

Third, the college will continue to use the instructional clinic with part-time personnel. The topics for 1979–80 are: competency-based module development, assessment of teaching effectiveness, and instructional practices designed to foster sex equity. Again, the state Division of Vocational-Technical Education will provide funding for part-time faculty participation. The instructional clinic has proven itself in the quest for parity of instruction. The clinic will be continued and will in time succeed.

Seventeen years ago Kuhns identified a challenge facing two-year colleges: "American junior colleges would be hard pressed to offer the wealth and variety of programs currently available were it not for the dedicated instruction provided by hundreds of part-time faculty members" (1963, p. 8). Her assessment remains valid today. The HJC model is designed to realized the potential of these dedicated professionals and, thereby, to continue to engage the challenge of a changing clientele and a new decade.

References

Annual Survey of Part-Time Faculty Services. (rev.ed.) Hagerstown, Md.: Hagerstown Junior College, Office of Instructional Affairs, 1977.

Friedlander, J. "Instructional Practices of Part-time and Full-time Faculty." *Community College Review,* 1979, *6* (3), 65–72.

Gleazer, E. J. *Directory of the American Association of Community, Junior, and Technical Colleges.* Washington, D.C.: American Association of Community and Junior Colleges, 1979.

Haddad, M., and Dickens, M. E. "Competencies for Part-Time Faculty: The First Step." *Community and Junior College Journal,* 1978, *49* (3), 22–24.

Kuhns, E. P. "Part-Time Faculty." *Junior College Journal,* 1963, *33* (5), 8–12.

Parsons, M. H. "The Instructional Clinic: Staff Development in Action," *Proceedings: Seventh International Institute on the Community College,* Sarnia, Ontario, Canada, Lambton College, 1976. ED 129 354.

Parsons, M. H. "New Faces on Campus: Instructional Development with Part-Time Faculty." Paper presented at the 59th Annual Convention of the American Association of Community and Junior Colleges, Chicago, May 1, 1979.

Smith, R. R. "Developmental Needs of Community College Adjunct Faculty." *Community/Junior College Research Quarterly,* 1977, *2* (1), 31–36.

Michael H. Parsons is dean of instructional affairs at Hagerstown Junior College in Hagerstown, Maryland. He holds the Ed.D degree in interdisciplinary higher education from Western Michigan University. He has been working with staff development for full- and part-time faculty for over a decade.

Part-time instructors now teach a large proportion of college classes; it's time they become full-fledged faculty members.

Making "What's-His-Face" Feel at Home: Integrating Part-Time Faculty

Richard D. Greenwood

Colleges having reached a point where the number of part-time faculty approaches or equals the number of full-time faculty—indeed, evening faculty often are primarily part-time instructors—it is curious that the routine means of dealing with full-time faculty are not even considered for part-time members. The amount of teaching accomplished outside the classroom, the importance of establishing a sense of belonging to the institution, and the need for basic services require little expansion; however, the extension of such considerations beyond full-time faculty members too often takes a back seat to the mundane administrative details that grow from making sure that 'What's-his-face" has a classlist, a desk copy of the text, and a shove in the direction of the classroom. In short, the shuffling that is common to the opening days of a semester gobbles up the "part-timers" and, while the system flows on, they are left out of the mainstream.

The fact that "most colleges rely on personal contacts, unsolicited applications, or 'word-of-mouth' recommendations for hiring"

(Bender and Hammons, 1972, p. 21) points to the source of the problem: part-time faculties tend to be treated in ways which do not begin to approach routine procedures. Having been hired in a somewhat random manner—even the most conscientious departments seldom convene committees to screen potential part-time teachers—it is easy to overlook anything that follows. The result is the creation of a class of faculty which is employed outside of the mainstream and essentially kept outside by virtue of the fact that integration is seldom attempted.

Comparison with Full-Time Faculty is Revealing

To appreciate fully the plight of part-time teachers, one needs only to compare the basic accommodations and avenues of information provided for full-time faculty to those provided for part-time personnel.

Office Space. While conditions vary, the provision of office space, shared or unshared, is made automatically for full-time faculty. Part-time faculty are seldom provided space outside of the classroom. When it is provided, it is not uncommon for the "bullpen" approach to be used. The thinking is simple: if a teacher is only teaching one fifth of a normal load, then he or she only needs one fifth of an office. The problem with such an approach is that although mathematically sound, it fails to meet the teacher-student needs for one-on-one contact and impairs the tutorial role of the instructor. In addition, the herd approach to office allocation is demeaning to the individual; it says implicitly "You do not rate privacy." What might be worse, the absence of a private office for part-time faculty members subliminally informs the students that their teachers have a second-rate status in the eyes of the college. This question of status becomes a more serious problem when dealing with nontraditional students who have come to relate the possession of space with success. Often unsure of their own fitness for academic pursuit, they are shaken when their fears are compounded by the administration's failure to invest an office in a faculty member.

Opportunity to Meet with Peers. Since full-time faculty maintain offices together, meet together, and often serve on committees together, peer contact is natural and free flowing. As part-timers, faculty members have little occasion to do more than pass in the mailroom. The absence of contact can only harm both the attitude of the part-time instructor and the academic program. By being kept in a social vacuum, the part-time teacher is denied the opportunity to enter the intellectual mainstream of the institution and is constrained to see himself as a separate entity without social status in the academic community. Even worse, the absence of social exchange takes away the opportunities for learning which are a byproduct of such exchange. The casual sharing of information in teaching methods, materials, and student problems ceases when faculty members are not provided an atmosphere that encourages the free exchange of academic information. In the absence of such sharing, the overall academic growth of faculty members is stunted.

A Voice in Planning and Operation of the Institution. Even before the advent of collective bargaining, it was common for faculty to play an active role in institutional planning and operation. While the arrival of collective bargaining may not have increased participation, it has codified it. The part-time faculty member has seldom had access to the decision-making processes which exist. Again, the result is exclusionary and the part-time faculty member is left with a sense of being severed from the life of the college community. He is given a sense of being acted upon without a voice in the direction.

What is made fairly obvious by such comparison is that part-time faculty members are put in a different academic environment than the one in which full-timers operate. Rather than being descriptive, it is proscriptive. Rather than being one which cultivates, it dominates. By failing to suggest that part-time faculty members are valued members of an academic family, such an environment sustains the image of part-time faculty as an expendable commodity which is allowed to circulate on the periphery but is not a wholly accepted member of the collegial world.

Finding a Solution

Having recognized that a problem exists, how can an institution with all of its needs and concerns initiate a course of action designed to ensure the socialization of its part-time faculty? Each problem area must be dealt with in accordance with the abilities of the institution and the priority it gives the problem.

The Committee. One method accomplishes several goals at the same time: by establishing a committee of part-time faculty members it is possible to concurrently give a voice to the part-timers and evaluate the shortcomings of the institution. Before beginning to use a committee, there are some significant considerations.

The Commitment. Any institution which is not committed to improving the lot of its part-time faculty should avoid attempting a superficial commitment to an advisory committee. Once the wheels are in motion, the pent-up suggestions and ideas should not be simply given lip service. If, however, the institution's commitment is genuine, the outpouring of reasonable ideas will be a vauable tool for initiating worthwhile change.

The Mix. Like any body, the committee will be most useful if the members represent the constituency and are willing to work with the administration in a cooperative spirit. This is not to suggest that the committee members should rubber stamp every idea the administration puts forth; but it is important to ensure that the committee will not get bogged down by individual "hobby-horses." Therefore, a good blend might consist of a couple of "old-timers" who are known for their willingness to help new instructors, some middle-term instructors (those who have been with the college for more than two years), and some new part-timers who have experienced particular problems in learning the ropes. At the same time, the committee should consist of representative individuals. Determinants could include sex, age, and professional objectives — the professional who is teaching because he enjoys the challenge of the classroom has different needs and insights than the part-time teacher who is teaching in order to survive until a full-time position becomes available.

The Charge. Because part-time faculty are not generally afforded the perspective of the institution's needs and goals, not to mention its idiosyncracies, it is crucial that the committee charge be stated in the clearest terms. Such a committee can remain a productive force only when it understands that it is an advisory, not legislative, body. Once the problems and needs discerned by the committee begin to be translated into administrative action, the question of the committee's usefullness will be answered.

Putting the Solution in Motion. Since the intent of establishing a committee of part-time faculty is to improve the sense of belonging and significance, the committee should be exposed to varied elements of the college's administrative team. A dinner meeting with the dean is a comfortable way to begin. Such a meeting reinforces the idea of the institution's resolve and recognition of the committee's purpose and import. Follow-up meetings with other members of the administration are valuable and productive.

Beyond meetings with selected personnel, the committee should be directed to address other important, albeit abstract, problems. First among these problems is the aforementioned syndrome of the part-timer as an outsider. Who can better evaluate the etiology and cure for the problem than those who have witnessed it first hand? The fact that it appears on the agenda will surely alert the committee members that the administration is concerned about part-time teachers and determined to integrate this body into the mainstream.

Toward Socialization. Once given the sense that the college is willing to hear the part-timer, the need for socialization should be attended to. The entire college should participate. Often the academic departments will eagerly respond to suggestions which involve meeting with part-time faculty members on an informal basis; cocktail parties, late afternoon coffees, special luncheons, all prove to be excellent means for full- and part-time faculty to meet and share common interests. It is also possible that the college senate, or whatever collegewide body is existent, might sponsor some get-together. The idea once suggested, it is a pleasant surprise to learn how many departments and faculty organizations are interested in participating in making the part-time staff feel like members of the college.

The need for socialization—even the most Dionysian faculty cannot stand up under the constant demand of cocktail parties forever—can be easily accomplished by setting up a lounge for part-time teachers. While faculty have their offices and established social patterns, the part-time teacher is offered few opportunities to relax and engage in conversation with his academic counterparts. Investing in a coffeepot and some comfortable furniture will provide valuable returns in the impact on faculty attitude and academic effectiveness. And the best thing about a lounge is that full-time faculty members gravitate to it: the result is a homogeneous mix of faculty joined in conversations which present learning experiences difficult to match with even the most sophisticated staff development program. Again, socialization at this level is not a difficult achievement either in money or effort.

Instilling a Sense of Value. The final element in the integration of part-time faculty is to provide them with facilities for meeting with students. While it would be ridiculous to suggest that an office be provided for every part-time teacher or even for every two members of the part-time faculty, it is not unreasonable to suggest providing some office and filing space. Again, the effort should be a cooperative one in which both the administration and the individual departments establish areas for use by part-time instructors. At Montgomery Community College the Office of Part-Time Studies has three offices and one room of file cabinets set aside for the exclusive use of part-time faculty. The offices are tastefully appointed—no bare walls and monastic furniture—and the files room is kept under strict security, guaranteeing the integrity of teaching and testing materials. In addition to the offices in the administrative area, there are offices scattered around the campus that are open evenings for use by the part-timer. The total number of offices does not come near the number of part-time teachers — a large number will be engaged in cocktail parties, coffee hours, or lounge discussions, anyway — and a ratio of one office for every twelve faculty is quite reasonable.

Putting It All Together

Once provision has been made for including part-time faculty in the decision-making process, bringing them into the social milieu of the institution, and establishing space for meeting with students and storing material, results will be gratifying. Backed by an informative handbook, one which discusses the part-time faculty committee and the attempts of the college to bring the part-time faculty into the fold, the entire program will produce far reaching benefits in the areas of faculty satisfaction and academic pride. If part-time faculty are handicapped by their employers, institutions can be assured they will respond in kind; but a sense of belonging and worth can be fostered if the institution steps forward and demonstrates its commitment to serving those who provide it the benefits of special expertise and flexibility. Failing to move toward socialization and participation will only perpetuate the idea that "part-time faculty" is no more than a euphemism for "what's-his-face, the temporary teacher."

Reference

Bender, L. W., and Hammons, J. O. "Adjunct Faculty: Forgotten and Neglected." *Community and Junior College Journal,* 1972, *43* (2), 20–22.

Richard D. Greenwood is the assistant dean of academic affairs and director of part-time studies at Montgomery County Community College, Blue Bell, Pennsylvania.

A community-based college can achieve its objectives by relying upon part-time faculty.

Utilizing Part-Time Faculty for Community-Based Education

Edward H. Decker

Within the past two decades the American two-year-college mission has experienced dramatic change. The junior college of the 1950s, with its primary purpose of providing transfer opportunities for some, is now the comprehensive community college for all. Programs for transfer, occupational training, and community service are offered in recognition of education's place in improving the quality of life and in fulfilling lifelong needs. As the American people enter "the learning society," the modern comprehensive community college is demonstrating its ability to move in step with rapid change.

A college title which includes the word *community* implies an intent to respond to the needs of the people in a local geographic region. With increasing mobility and advancing technologies causing the expansion of people's horizons, the concepts of community, neighborhood, and family are being eroded. Organizations and experiences which strengthen these fundamental American concepts are important to balance the strains of modernization—community colleges fit this description.

Social Commitment

The mission has continued to evolve, however, and many community colleges have achieved the advanced level of becoming community-based, comprehensive colleges. This accelerates the concept that the college does not only exist for its community but its goals and programs are shaped by the community. Community-based colleges are educational institutions with a social commitment.

An experience which brought this concept to life for me may serve to illustrate the point.

About fourteen years ago, while serving as an instructor with Oakland Community College in Michigan, I had an opportunity to participate in a discussion involving representatives of the college and local communities. The college was new and the citizens were curious about its purpose. Eventually, the discussion focused on the term "community," and one citizen asked why the college name included the word. John E. Tirrell, college president, answered that Oakland would strive to be the community's college, striving to meet the educational and cultural needs of the community college district. He continued by stressing that the true goal of any community college is "to help its community achieve self-actualization."

Tirrell's words have served as a constant reminder of the essential purpose of community colleges. The vision is very special: an educational institution catering to the learning wants and wishes of its taxpayers. Can such an unheard-of dream become reality? Can occupational programs be developed to provide qualified graduates for new job opportunities, then modified or eliminated as the job market shifts? Will institutional research methods be designed to identify true local community needs? Can tenured faculty be retrained to meet new instructional demands? Will established departments and divisions, curriculum committees, and academic senates be capable of change?

Reaching the Geographic Community

One promising approach to achieving community-based higher education is the noncampus college, a concept operating in a half-dozen U.S. communities. To counter the complexities of travel, parking, and crowds; to respond to societal demands of convenience and cost reductions; to recognize that knowledge is a portable commodity not dependent on ivy-walled sanctuaries, the noncampus college is a realistic way to bring knowledge into neighborhoods and homes.

Coastline Community is such a college. Now in its third year of operation, Coastline serves coastal Orange County, California, in the rapidly growing corridor between Los Angeles and San Diego. When Coastline was launched, Norman Watson, chancellor of the Coast Community College District (of which Coastline is a member), indicated that the purpose of Coastline is to offer educational programs to the community in new ways. Now, with its novel organizational structure centered around geographical areas and part-time faculty and with its people-oriented research methods, Coastline has reached beyond those early goals and is achieving community-based education.

The district Coastline serves is 105 miles of Pacific Coast real estate with more than 550,000 people. The area also includes Golden West and Orange Coast Colleges, two large comprehensive campus-based community colleges. The three schools comprise Coast Community College District.

When formed, Coastline was given responsibility for all off-campus instruction previously operated by the district's evening division. With high schools, churches, and community centers already in use throughout the district, it was immediately clear that Coastline's organizational structure would have to conquer distance.

The idea of an organization structured by geographic areas rather than discipline-oriented divisions was conceived by Coastline's president, Bernard Luskin. The goals are community interaction and immediacy. The college must be prepared to respond promptly and relevantly to community needs, and to strive to become an intimate part of each municipality. Four geographic areas were identified and it was decided that each area would be headed by a new position, an area administrator who would be strategically located in his or her area.

Community-Based Faculty

Coastline's commitment to a community base is exemplified in more ways than the geographic area structure. To be community based means more than outreach; it also means finding ways to bring community relevance and wisdom into the mainstream of college activity.

On a typical evening at Estancia High School in Costa Mesa, thirty Coastline classes are offered. Students from surrounding neighborhoods arrive to receive instruction in Spanish, real estate appraisal, insurance, marketing, and painting. The instructors are not full-time contract faculty but instead are lawyers, real estate brokers, and craftsmen who choose to spend some time each week sharing their knowledge with others. Coastline's Estancia coordinator, Al Matz, who also serves as an assistant principal for the high school, recently remarked that it is edifying to listen to the students praise their instructors for the high degree of quality and relevance, and very comforting to see the facilities in maximum use: a community high school by day; a community college by night.

All but a handful of Coastline's 800 faculty members are part time, hired as needed on an hourly basis, and earning between fourteen and nineteen dollars per hour for the time they are in the classroom. (Coastline has 42 percent of the part-time faculty in the three-college district.)

Although intensive use of part-time faculty is not essential to the overall concept of the college, it does help tailor an ever-changing curriculum to the needs of the community.

Coastline benefits greatly from the ability to draw from an extensive talent pool for its faculty. The college has many more applications for positions than it has positions available. About 30 percent of its instructors teach full time at other higher education institutions. Another 20 percent are full-time high school teachers. Of the others, many are employed in business and industry and teach subjects allied to their own professions. Still others have left full-time teaching through retirement, family commitments, or layoff due to declining secondary school enrollments. All, however, are fully credentialed and, since hiring is based on college district personnel standards, meet the same criteria as faculty at the Coast district's campus institutions.

Faculty morale is high at Coastline where, unlike many other institutions, the part-time instructor "sits at the head of the table." During its second year of operation, faculty members organized an academic senate, overturning an antiquated state prohibition against the formation of such a panel of part-time faculty. The senate serves as the faculty voice in matters of professional and academic concern.

The special needs of the part-time faculty are foremost in the minds of the college administrators. Instructional services are designed, from the ground up, to assist the part-time faculty member—everything from photocopying of instructional materials and speedy delivery of audiovisual gear to teaching sites to professional staff development enterprise.

Instead of the traditional series of departmental faculty meetings, Coastline's faculty confer at social evenings built around themes like "Motivating the Adult Learner." Faculty often bring their spouses and stay after conclusion of the formal program. Faculty are made to feel like "one of the family." They are granted recognition through the college newsletter, *The Coast-Liner,* and other types of publicity. As one faculty member, who also teaches evenings for a nearby university, put it, "I do a better job at Coastline because the people there care about what I'm doing. In my other class, I feel like a second-class citizen."

Some members of Coastline's community based faculty are:

- Alan: He is a personnel manager for one of the nation's largest yacht and recreational vehicle builders. Alan is an instructor of employee benefits administration in Coastline's personnel associate program.
- Christine: She operates a riding stable located on the Newport Beach Bay and teaches equestrian courses for Coastline.
- Don: He is an experienced banker and a leader among the local banking community. He is an instructor in the principles of banking operations.
- Larry: He is a real estate broker who specializes in commercial and industrial real estate. He is an instructor of real estate principles with Coastline.
- Lee: She owns and operates her own travel agency serice and is a recognized leader in the field. She is an instructor of travel agency courses.
- Pete: He serves as manager of a large, luxury apartment complex in Newport Beach. He teaches property management classes for Coastline.
- Sam: He has seventeen years of experience in city government and currently serves as the director of community services for the city of Westminster. Sam is an instructor of management supervision courses.

The above examples are but a few of the many ways in which Coastline is taking advantage of community experts to incorporate its educational commitment. Through continued refinement of this use of community experts on a part-time basis, Coastline Community College will bring reality to the elusive dream of community-based education.

Edward H. Decker is dean of instruction at Coastline Community College in Orange County, California He holds the Ph.D. degree from Michigan State University and has been a community college teacher and administrator in three state systems.

Financial assistance is available to conduct in-service training when community colleges work cooperatively with their state agencies.

Support for Training Vocational-Technical Adjunct Faculty

Joseph P. DeSantis

The increased reliance on adjunct faculty for teaching occupational courses in Maryland's community colleges is a well-documented fact. Data collected and maintained by the Division of Vocational-Technical Education (DVTE), Maryland State Department of Education, support the conclusion reached by Lombardi (1975) that part-time instructors now form the majority of all instructors in the community colleges. Yet, there is no existing state support for a systemwide approach to provide inservice training for the part-time vocational-technical instructors who are teaching an increasing number of students.

This problem was recognized at the spring 1978 meeting of community college administrators responsible for occupational programs. Designated as the Occupational Deans and Directors Group, membership is extended to the chief community college vocational-technical administrator and representatives from state agencies that have an impact on vocational-technical education. The director of programs from the State Board for Community Colleges (SBCC) and the executive director for the State Advisory Council for Vocational-Technical Education (SACVE) serve as ex-officio members. Staff support to the group is provided by the DVTE specialist in Postsecondary and Adult Education, who serves as executive secretary.

The topic of vocational-technical faculty required discussion because of increased reliance by Maryland's two-year institutions on teachers who have vocational expertise but relatively little training in teaching methods or objectives. Since Maryland does not require certification for teaching occupational subjects at the postsecondary level, recruitment is based primarily on the individual's experience in a certain occupation. Training in pedagogy is secondary. Orientation upon appointment is minimal and consists primarily of textbook identification, course syllabus, and some general "housekeeping" rules.

No uniform pattern for assisting the adjunct vocational-technical instructor to improve effectiveness was identified among the colleges. Rather, each institution proceeds independently to recruit, orient, and evaluate its part-time faculty using whatever campus resources it can marshal for these purposes.

The financial burdens imposed by high-cost occupational programs are alleviated by employment of part-time faculty. This additionally creates flexibility in the time schedules of full-time vocational-technical faculty. Despite these advantages, little is being done to improve the instructional productivity of this critically needed human resource. The 1978 meeting addressed the problems of determining the adjunct faculty member's needs for inservice training and finding financial sources for meeting them. "What role could be played by the individual colleges, state agencies, and national vocational organizations in supporting inservice training for this select group of faculty?" was the persistent question.

Financial Assistance

Once schools with limited resources were faced by the need to successfully combine the adjunct faculty member's contribution to the occupational program and his professional growth, financial necessity was a stimulus for exploring possible outside sources of assistance. Under existing legislation, only one state agency is identified as the recipient of federal funds to support vocational education at both the secondary and postsecondary levels. In Maryland, the State Department of Education is the designated state agency. Program responsibility for the use of this money, in accordance with federal rules and regulations, is vested in the Division of Vocational-Technical Education, a specialized instructional unit within the department. Title II, Vocational Education Public Law 94-482, provides categorical monies for program support and for improving the qualifications of personnel serving in vocational education programs. Under Section 104.774 of the Federal Rules and Regulations, monies may be used by the recipient state to support projects of inservice training in methods of instruction for vocational education teachers. Through an extensive planning and review process, Maryland provided funds in its FY 1979 Annual State Plan for establishing a state exemplary system to assist in development of a vocational-technical instructional program.

Once the decision was made by the occupational deans and directors to establish a statewide professional development plan (subject to outside funding) for adjunct vocational-technical faculty, the DVTE staff specialist in Postsecondary and Adult Education took measures to incorporate the proposed activity into Maryland's plan for exemplary projects eligible for federal funding at the postsecondary level.

The standard project format to be followed consisted of major sections commencing with "Statement of Need" and culminating with the proposed "Budget." The responsibility for conducting the proposed workshops would be assumed by the college submitting the proposal.

Cooperative Steps

Hagerstown Junior College (HJC) was identified as submitter of the project. Proposal design became the responsibility of the associate dean of instructional services who also serves as local plan coordinator for vocational-technical education. At HJC the dean's efforts resulted in the establishment of a partnership with Prince George's Community College. This divided the state into two regions and made workshops more accessible. Each of the two community colleges hosted a Saturday workshop on its campus. Cooperative effort gave additional support to designation of the project as "exemplary," thus qualified for the federal funds allocated in the state plan.

One of the key components of the submitted proposal was support from the state's Western Maryland Resource Center (WMRC) located in Allegany County. Full-time staff of the center would videotape the inservice activities at both college locations. The taping supports Ward's (1972) findings of increased reliance on electronic equipment for inservice training.

Encouragement was given by paying travel expenses plus a fifty dollar stipend for attendance at the all-day session. Enthusiastic response corresponded to that experienced by a New Jersy community college which also offered remuneration.

The proposal called for an interest inventory to determine needs as perceived by the adjunct faculty. The compiled results served as the basis of the agenda for the workshops. Again, campus wide cooperative efforts among the participating community colleges strengthened the professional bond existing among the college administrators.

The project evaluation and final report were completed in accordance with the proposal plan. Copies of each videotaped presentation were placed with the Western Maryland Resource Center for issuance upon request. A number of Maryland's colleges had duplicate tapes made so they could be shown at local inservice meetings.

An unexpected outcome was the opportunity for the project director to participate in a forum on inservice training held as part of the 1979 American Association of Community and Junior Colleges Conference in Chicago. As a result, community college personnel in numerous states requested copies of the video cassettes, and evidence of the need for materials to support inservice training for adjunct faculty increased. (Since funds were not provided for this purpose in the initial low-cost budget, no formal attempts have been made to assess the effectiveness of video materials outside Maryland.)

A major outcome of the Maryland effort has been the design of a model built through the cooperation of seventeen diverse institutions from both rural and urban areas. Strong leadership from college administrators in both design and implementation ensured local acceptance of the model from full- and part-time vocational-technical faculty. At the state level support extended beyond the financial commitment of approximately $8,000. Other state assistance included media personnel and equipment and the inclusion of all workshop print and video materials in the circulation network maintained by DVTE.

Future Efforts

Experiences gained from Maryland's first statewide effort to conduct structured workshops for inservice training of adjunct faculty provided the basis for a cooperative venture involving the National Alliance of Postsecondary Education Institutions/Districts. Member institutions collaborate to solve common educational problems using their combined resources. Federal funds, awarded by formula grant to

Maryland's two-year institutions, are being committed on a voluntary basis by administrators to support membership costs in the alliance. Future inservice activities developed through this association will be shared among all the colleges.

Within Maryland, continuing education administrators involved with recruitment, orientation, and inservice training of adjunct faculty who teach non-credit courses have expressed an interest in a statewide meeting with occupational deans and directors. A major agenda item will be the exploration of ways in which cooperation could be fostered between the credit vocational-technical programs conducted under community services sponsorshop. Sharing resources of these programs, especially in faculty development workshops, could lead to a strengthening of the vocational education available to Maryland residents.

References

Lombardi, J. *Part-Time Faculty in Community Colleges.* Topical Paper No. 54. Los Angeles: ERIC Clearinghouse for Junior Colleges, 1975. (ED 115 316)

Maryland State Department of Education. *Maryland State Plan for Vocational-Technical Education.* Baltimore: Division of Vocational-Technical Education, 1979.

Ward, G. *A Review of Literature and Research on Inservice Training for Teachers with Emphasis on Vocational and Technical Teachers.* Stillwater: Oklahoma State Department of Vocational and Technical Education, Division on Research, Planning, and Evaluation, 1972. (ED 073 244)

Joseph P. DeSantis is a specialist in postsecondary and adult education, Division of Vocational-Technical Education in Maryland. Prior to this assignment, he served as a community college administrator in three state systems.

An examination of the legal and administrative issues
related to "mainstreaming" of part-time faculty
has become imperative in an era of declining
enrollments and faculty retrenchment.

Mainstreaming Part-Time Faculty: Issue or Imperative?

Louis S. Albert
Rollin J. Watson

The use of part-time faculty is one of the most potentially volatile issues in higher education today because of the conflict between the obligation of institutions to simultaneously provide high quality learning environments and operate within present-day financial constraints. As college enrollments decline and budgets tighten, both faculty members and administrators are scrutinizing part-time employment practices. The debate is not just over the question of whether a part-time faculty is a cushion against retrenchment, as some administrators claim, or whether hiring part-timers is a way to avoid the expense of full-time positions, as some faculty members contend. The practice of employing part-time teachers had direct impact upon the entire educational process. Among the most significant issues to be identified are the emerging legal issues and related administrative concerns regarding part-time faculty. These issues must be dealt with if the part-time faculty is to indeed be integrated into the academic processes of an institution.

Debate Over Part-Time Faculty Utilization

Increasing use of part-time faculty in institutions that can no longer afford to add full-time faculty has led to considerable criticism of the trend on pedagogical, financial, and legal levels. The American Association of University Professors (AAUP) and the American Federation of Teachers (AFT) are alarmed by what they call a "dramatic rise" in the use of part-time faculty. The unions denounce the over-employment of part-timers because it exploits those who teach part-time at the same time it undermines salaries and benefits of full-time faculty members (Magarrell, 1978). The AAUP also contends that part-time faculty members are generally less qualified, offer few non-teaching services, and do not contribute to the institution's reputation (Magarrell, 1978). One author suggested that the desire of some part-time faculty members to achieve tenure has created a competition between part- and full-timers which works in favor of administrators and boards of trustees (Koltai, 1977).

In spite of these negative aspects of part-time-faculty employment, it is increasing for the following reasons:

- The per-course-rate makes pay lower for part-time faculty than full-time faculty salaries.
- Part-time faculty receive no fringe benefits.
- Minimal office space is required.
- Part-time faculty can be hired on a course-by-course basis with no long-term commitments.
- Part-time teachers provide great flexibility in providing instruction in emerging disciplines.

There is some disagreement over whether part-time faculty members are underpaid in comparison with full-time. The AFT claimed that part-time and adjunct faculty members are often paid at rates "ranging down to one third or less of established salaries scales," ("Increasing Use . . . ," 1977), but a study done for the AAUP showed that when adjustments are made to reflect time spent on nonteaching duties of full-time faculty members, parity in part-time and full-time pay is apparent (Magarrell, 1978). Of course, the question of what constitutes "full-time" status has never been completely answered. Definition is more to the advantage of the faculty member now in a time of retrenchment than it was earlier when outside sources of income were plentiful. At that time, it was the administrators who were calling for clearer definitions of what constituted "full-time status" (Williams, 1965).

Major Legal Issues

Because of the pressure being exerted on both sides, some disruptive legal issues have emerged, including the issue of tenure for part-time faculty. The California Court of Appeals handed down a landmark decision in a suit by the Peralta Federation of Teachers, Local 1603, against the Peralta Community College District. Twelve part-time teachers employed by the district sought writ of mandate to grant them tenure and to compensate them at a rate equivalent to full-time faculty. The court ruled that those instructors who carried 60 percent or more of a full-time load could be eligible for tenure (Koltai, 1977).

Traditionally, part-time faculty members have been thought of as "moonlighters," but the exclusivity of this concept is under challenge. One of the strongest advocates of an expanded notion of part-time teaching is the feminist movement, which proposes that part-time employees be given all of the benefits, opportunites, and responsibilities that they would receive as full-time employees. The proposal would in effect, be a compromise between those who see part-time employment as exploitation and those who claim it is a product of financial exigency. While seeing some justification for "moonlighter" part-time appointments, feminist groups would like to see "sunlight" part-time appointments.

These would be "regular faculty appointments, alike in every way to full-time faculty, except the amount of time worked. These persons receive prorated fringe benefits, committee assignments, advisees, tenure and, sabbatical accrual" (Part-Time Faculty Employment . . . , 1976, p. 2). Purportedly, this kind of appointment would benefit working parents and enhance the professionalism of part-time faculties.

Developing Institutional Policy

An interesting analysis of part-time-faculty contracts was made by a former community college dean in Maryland. One of the points he made is that institutions should include a statement in the contract that time spent as a part-time employee will not be used toward tenure. He also warns that institutions should not offer more than 49 percent of a full-time position to a part-time instructor. In addition to dates, times, and salary, a good contract should include the following statements: a "policies and procedures" manual is explicitly subsumed, the contract does not provide for future commitment or priority, and part-time instructors must meet standards of performance. The contract should spell out all requirements that must be met by the instructor, advising and office hour requirements, and the instructor's obligation with regard to grading policy and submission of grades (Van Winkle, 1978).

In addition, a fairness doctrine for the hiring of part-time professors should be subscribed to by institutions of higher education. Market realities — a surplus of qualified, "hungry" teachers combined with shrinking budgets — militate against the refinement of part-time appointments as described earlier; but for the good of both students and the profession, faculty and administrators should work toward a rational policy for hiring part-time instructors. Institutions should develop policies regarding part-time faculty, and they should work toward eliminating the abuses which have become traditional at certain institutions and in some departments (for example, hiring of chairman's friends). Part-time faculty contracts should be drawn up by a lawyer. A due process system should be developed for use in termination cases and this should include a fair evaluation and adequate warning of impending termination.

A Case in Point. Unfortunately, many colleges receive meager legal advice and are usually at "ground zero" in the development of legally sufficient part-time faculty policies and procedures. At a community college in the East, where the percentage of part-time faculty members has increased 47 percent (virtually matching the increase in part-time students over the past four years), the failure of attention to certain legal questions was brought to the college's notice by a part-time faculty member. Just before the fall semester opened, one department hired a graduate student to teach an introductory course. The contract signed by the instructor had no termination clause. When numerous charges of poor teaching were received, the division chairman went to the instructor's classroom to talk with the students and found the situation so bad that he decided, with concurrence of the associate dean, to relieve the instructor of his duties immediately. The instructor sought legal counsel, who advised that since the contract contained no termination clause and since the college had given no opportunity for due process, the instructor should sue the college for defamation of character, if, in fact, he was formally discharged from his teaching responsibilities. The contract appointing the instructor had stated a definite rank for a specified period of time. Rather than go to court, the college decided to pay the instructor for the rest of the semester and remove any mention of termination from his record. The college determined that, although it could provide evidence of the instructor's lack of ability to teach, it had not provided him warning prior to his suspension from the classroom or review thereafter. Furthermore, because it had not been signed by the president of the college, there was a question whether the contract was binding.

And Some Benefits. Simultaneous with the incident discussed above, members of the full-time faculty of the same institution were beginning to complain about the failure of the college to maintain the same ratio of part- and full-time faculty members that it had in its early years. It became obvious to the administration that it must inaugurate a comprehensive policy on the part-time faculty. This system was developed in conjunction with a revised part-time-faculty handbook which described the contractual obligations of the part-time faculty member and of the institution.

The college's new policy on part-time instructors had to consider four points — all common in termination cases — raised by the dismissal dispute: (1) the authority to make contracts (the contested contract signed by the instructor was not countersigned by a high-level official of the college); (2) implications of contractual obligations of public versus private institutions; (3) due process requirements (in the example discussed, the instructor was given no opportunity for review of the case presented against him); and (4) the instructor's First Amendment rights (Rood, 1977).

Integrating Legal, Administrative, and Institutional Issues

Having given some consideration to legal and administrative issues, institutions can turn to their true concern, the effective utilization of part-time instructors. It is important that administrators, if they are to improve the quality of performance of their part-time instructors, seek the involvement of full-time faculty members. With appropriate administrative and legal guidelines, part-time faculty should be incorporated to the greatest extent possible into the mainstream of the academic process. One of the outcomes of making adjunct faculty a part of the institution is the potential for keeping students. In dealing with financial problems caused by decreasing enrollment, institutions are increasingly turning their attention from focus on student recruitment to the problem of student retention, and an effective part-time faculty can prevent students from dropping out because of frustration with "the system."

Several fallacies and misconceptions regarding teaching part time point up the need for further research: It is too convenient to use that body of individuals as a scapegoat in the matter of student attrition. Are part-time teachers only in it for the money? Surveys indicate that this is true for only a small percentage of them. Do part-time faculty members give more high grades? There is some evidence that they do; however, this may indicate the institution's failure to clarify grading standards to members of part-time staff. The fact that part-timers teach more adult students may also have a bearing on this situation. Do they neglect the advising role of the teacher? If they do, it may be because institutions have not provided the means of improving their service to the students.

At Essex Community College, in Baltimore County, Maryland, a collegewide retention committee concluded that one of the causes of student attrition was that part-time faculty made inadequate use of college resources and rarely referred students with problems to appropriate college offices. The student-retention committee recommended that the office of the dean of instruction look more closely at student attrition in classes taught by part-time faculty and attempt to develop an orientation and follow-up program for part-time teachers which would meet these deficiencies.

There are many other aspects of part-time instruction which could be causes of student attrition (part-time faculty recruitment and selection, the quality of part-time teaching, limited interaction between part-time and full-time faculty members). Only limited results can be achieved in a single orientation session. Although multiple sessions might be useful, part-time contracts do not contain an obligation to participate in such sessions, and the college could not afford to provide incentive through additional pay. Furthermore, part-time faculty usually hold full-time jobs in other locations, so scheduling of orientation sessions would be extremely difficult. The problem is complicated and deserves a careful solution.

A plan should evolve from the needs of the institution with the primary consideration being quality of teaching. Such a plan, therefore, should involve the following:

- Making a full, fair consideration of legal issues inherent in part-time employment.
- Making the faculty and administrative staff aware of the problems and seeking their involvement.
- Bringing about interaction between full-time and part-time faculty.

- Helping the part-time faculty to use the system of resources available by providing adequate orientation and follow-up.
- Obtaining useful data on the effectiveness of part-time instruction.
- Providing continuing support for the part-time faculty.

The first step an institution must take is to make its own staff aware of problems with part-time faculty. One of the dangers of having a central office administer part-time faculty is that they then have virtually no contact with individuals and departments with whom they are working. Decentralization, the involvement of divisions and departments in the hiring, orientation, and evaluation of instructors, can be especially helpful.

The most important component of the plan discussed earlier is number four, helping part-time faculty use the system of resources which already exists for full-time faculty. This involves an orientation program, a set of written policies and procedures, and a sufficient amount of space and equipment for part-time faculty to do an adequate job of teaching and advising students.

An effective orientation program should describe teaching methods and college resources. Each institution must decide whether general faculty orientation meetings followed by divisional meetings are more satisfactory than solely departmental meetings which use materials developed by the administration. In either case, orientation should be structured and pursued.

One benefit of the orientation meeting should be increased interaction between members of the full- and part-time faculties. Institutions which have grown too large must personalize the process so that part-time faculty members will begin to identify themselves with a department or division of the college. The exchange of information among colleagues will be helpful in teaching.

Schools can no longer afford to treat part-time faculty as mere adjuncts. It is time to regard part-time faculty members as professional educators, even if their primary allegiance is to another profession. They must be allowed to develop professionally in the same ways full-time faculty are. To this end, they must be permitted access to the "system" and be encouraged to take advantage of it to improve the job they are doing.

Mainstreaming the part-time faculty is no longer an issue; it is an imperative. Part-time instruction cannot and should not replace instruction by full-time educators. However, to the greatest extent possible, part-time teaching should be a continuation of the full-time faculty's activity, enhancing and reinforcing the goals of the full-time faculty. The role of the part-time faculty should be carefully spelled out by institutions so that use of such persons enhances rather than detracts from the quality of collegiate instruction. Since the part-time faculty is here to stay, it must flow with the mainstream of academic endeavor in colleges and universities. Part-time teachers, like full-time instructors, are professional educators with an important role to play in higher education.

References

"Increasing Use of Part-Time Condemned by Teachers' Union." *Chronicle of Higher Education,* 1977, *15,* 4.

Koltai, L. "King Solomon and the Bowl of Spaghetti." *Community and Junior College Journal,* 1977, *48,* 20.

Magarrell, J. "Part-Time Professors on the Increase." *Chronicle of Higher Education,* 1978, *15,* 1.

Part-Time Faculty Employment. Project on the Status and Education of Women. Washington, D.C.: Association of American Colleges, 1976. (ED 167 022.)

Rood, H. J. "Legal Issues in Faculty Termination." *Journal of Higher Education,* 1977, *68,* 124.

Van Winkle, R. A. *Analysis of Part-Time Contract Information.* Bel Air, Md.: Harford Community College, 1978.

Williams, L. *The Administration of Academic Affairs in Higher Education.* Ann Arbor: University of Michigan Press, 1965.

Louis S. Albert is dean of instruction at Essex Community College in Baltimore County, Maryland. He is known for his work in allied health program development and is a candidate for a Ph.D. in Higher Education at the University of Maryland.

Rollin J. Watson is associate dean of instruction, continuing education and community services at Essex. He holds a Ph.D. in American studies from the University of Maryland and has done postdoctoral study at John Hopkins University.

There are two sides to the adjunct faculty story.
An adjunct tells his experiences.

Observations of an Adjunct Faculty Member

Richard R. Beman

For nearly thirty years I have been an adjunct to several institutions of higher learning. My purpose in this chapter is to express a viewpoint and provide some insights which may be interesting and even useful to those who have not worked as a part-time, or adjunct, member of the faculty.

There is no way for me to know whether or not my experiences are typical because one of the problems is that adjuncts rarely know each other unless they happen to work together. There is no unifying group spirit. The usual communication is from college and university administrators, although we occasionally speak with faculty members who are directly involved in a course we are teaching.

Of course adjuncts have some things in common, particularly if a division is made between part- and full-time adjuncts. Hitherto the terms "adjunct" and "part-time" faculty were more or less synonymous. The use of full-time adjuncts is a fairly recent development which arose in response to the institutions' financial need. The full-time adjunct may have the same course load as a regular faculty member but no prospect of tenure, no fringe benefits, and an income of one third to one half that of his more secure colleagues.

My own experience relates to an entirely different group. These people teach part time, usually in the field in which they work full time. An example would be a clinical psychologist who earns his living as a therapist and teaches abnormal psychology. On one hand, these adjuncts probably have less graduate credits and degrees than their full-time teaching colleagues, though there are conspicuous exceptions to this generalization. On the other hand, experience in non-academic areas, such as management and health care, is likely to be much greater. Institutions are glad to make use of this experience to bring their instruction up-to-date. It is inevitable that faculty teaching full time will grow out-of-touch with changes in the workday world (Parsons, 1979). (Some adjuncts are full-time researchers and thus in possession of the latest information in a particular area.)

The distinctions which keep us separated from regular faculty members are many and varied. In my own field, management, there are some practical and ideological conflicts which are especially interesting. Both sides are guilty. There is a viewpoint widely held in the business world that academe generally harbors people who are harmlessly inept or dangerously brilliant. An exception was made for specialties recognized to be useful, and acceptance is accelerating as the demand grows for people competent in specific technologies. For their part, many school administrators are misinterpreting the signals they are receiving from the job market. As an example, advertisements for management faculty are likely to read: "Earned doctorate required, some experience helpful." From the academic point of view this denigration of experience is understandable. Unfortunately, it serves as another way of belittling the usefulness of adjuncts and it hurries the time of reckoning with student consumers.

Students are becoming increasingly insistent on the relevance of education to career opportunities and will become skeptical of the instructor who is unable to relate his subject to the world of work. The growing number of students who are employees will sharpen the focus of this problem.

Another paradox is that adjuncts are held to a higher standard of performance than full-time faculty. The basic contract between the adjunct and the institution which he serves is for a single semester. If he fails to perform satisfactorily, his teaching for that institution ends. By contrast, the tenured faculty member who ceases to function properly often continues on the payroll. The treatment of the adjunct is fair if his employment is perceived as an extension of the private sector where nonperformance usually brings termination or early retirement. Moreover, it is in the tradition of the early universities, although then students were the boss. Now administrators make the decision to hire or fire, but students nevertheless show their judgment of an instructor when they enroll in or boycott his class.

The most common problem for the adjunct is the relative difficulty of communication. Unlike the regular faculty, he does not have lunch, coffee breaks, and casual conversation with colleagues or administrators. Being set apart from this community, he can expect to receive requests for information several days after the deadline for furnishing it. To illustrate, I was once given a mailbox two hours drive away, which I was presumably expected to check several times a week.

It is time to ask why an otherwise sane person would be an adjunct. It is clearly not a road to riches or prestige. I can only respond to the question in a very personal way: I like to teach. More specifically, I find a significant degree of satisfaction in the belief, however questionable, that I have something worthwhile to share with students. This belief is occasionally reinforced by response from a student which indicates he has gained something of interest and value. One of my students, who also did military personnel work, was confronted by a problem which he later recounted to me. A young couple, both in the military, had recently had a stillborn child. Their emotional problems were compounded by accusations from relatives that one or the other of the parents was responsible. They came in tears to my student who decided that since he had never dealt with a situation like this, he would have nothing to lose by trying some of Carl Rogers' interviewing techniques which we had discussed in class. With genuine amazement, he reported to me that the techniques worked. Experiences of this sort are rare, but they are what makes me teach.

If the relationship with students is one reward of teaching—Highet calls it "the happiness of making something" (1950, p. 10)—the other comes from the need to maintain a degree of mastery in my own field. Without it, I cannot give students current, correct information. The result is that both my job and teaching are more stimulating.

In balance, the rewards of teaching as an adjunct far outweigh the annoyances. I will continue teaching as long as students and administrators need me.

84

References

Highet, G. *The Art of Teaching.* New York: Random House, 1950.
Parsons, M. H. "Back To The Salt Mines—Career Faculty Returning to Industry." Paper commissioned for the sumer conference on Staff Development at the University of Texas, Austin, and the 10th Annual International Institute on the Community College at Lambton College, Sarnia, Ontario, Canada, 1979.

Richard R. Beman is personnel and safety manager for Certain-Teed Corporation in Williamsport, Maryland, and serves as an adjunct to a community college and a university in management subjects.

What can community colleges do to realize
part-time faculty potential? This chapter
summarizes the possibilities.

Future Directions:
Eight Steps to Parity
for Part-Time Faculty

Michael H. Parsons

What do the 1980s portend for America's two-year colleges? The experts are undecided; the chancellor of one of the nation's largest community college districts instructs us to "adapt to an uncertain future" (Koltai and Erickson, 1979–80, p. 9). A leading researcher informs us that "the practices of higher education are increasingly incompatible with our purposes" (Cross, 1979, p. 4). It is clear, however, that the old strategies will not meet the needs of students or part-time teachers.

A comprehensive review of the literature regarding part-time faculty and the material contained in this volume suggests that specific action is needed. The following eight-step plan is one way to develop the potential of part-time faculty. The community college will reap a twofold harvest from this development. The new student consumer will recognize parity of instruction and be a satisfied customer willing to buy more services and the potential of the part-time faculty will be brought to fruition, thereby strengthening the two year-college to meet the challenges of the 1980s.

The first step in the process requires movement from a passive to an active stance in obtaining the best part-time personnel available. Too many colleges accept those individuals who apply to teach, making no systematic effort to recruit until an emergency arises. The process of obtaining qualified, competent part-time faculty must be organized. Local businesses and industries need to be contacted, school systems screened, and advisory committees encouraged to recommend people. Once identified, qualified personnel must be oriented to the teaching requirements of the college. A variety of designs are available; workshops, mentor systems, and teaching clinics have proven effective. The result of successful recruitment and orientation is a cadre of dependable part-time teachers attuned to the college's mission.

Step two is the development of a contract that articulates college requirements while safeguarding part-time-teacher rights. In our increasingly litigious society it is important that agreements entered into with part-time personnel be based on sound legal principles. College requirements must be specified and instructor rights guaranteed. Attention to detail is mandated and legal consultation may be indicated.

Current compensation schedules for part-time personnel do not reflect the important role that they play in achieving the institution's mission. Step three is the design of a system that creates closer parity. While increased remuneration in a time of shrinking resources is not easy, the result will be higher morale among part-time teachers and greater identification with institutional goals.

Virtually all two-year colleges will be seeking increased racial and sexual equality during the 1980s. Affirmative action plans can be materially improved through the use of part-time faculty. Systematic needs analysis and targeted recruitment to achieve sex equity comprise step four. Further, increased heterogeneity among the part-time faculty will broaden role mode potential and improve instruction.

Integration of part-time faculty into the fabric of the institution is critical in achieving instructional parity, and to do this, a system including support services and communications networks is essential. Office space, audio-visual services, clerical assistance, identification cards, mail boxes, and instructional supplies are necessary if part-time teachers are to achieve their potential. Communications networks, including "buddy-systems," workshops, and involvement in divisional activities, link part-time faculty with the group life of the college. Step five is the development of a support services/communications network tailored to a college's needs.

Once part-time faculty have become part of the college's system of instruction, their impact on the teaching-learning process must be assessed. Step six calls for an evaluation design that provides review to individual part-time teachers and compares them as a group with their full-time colleagues. A mix of institutionally and commercially developed instruments has proven successful. At Hagerstown Junior College, local norms have been established for an in-house instrument over a six-year period. The design has proven efficient in relaying student appraisal to individual teachers. On several occasions the college has used the instructional development and effectiveness assessment (IDEA) system prepared by Kansas State University with all full- and part-time teachers to compare profiles. The results have given direction to development efforts. Other colleges have had success with the Student Instructional Report (SIR) system from Educational Testing Service. Whatever approach is selected, attention to evaluation and structured review is essential.

Step seven is designed to increase college impact on various new clientele in its service area. Part-time faculty move in professional circles outside of their responsibility with the college. If they are informed of college goals and committed to them, they can serve as valuable links with the community. Information can be passed through them to target groups to which they have access; they can recruit among potential students not easily accessible to regular college staff; and they can explain the college's mission to people who are unaware of available services. This function is the direct result of steps four and five above and pays substantial dividends.

The final step is the development of college/state cooperation to foster part-time-faculty development. Every state has a series of bureaus or departments charged with educational development. Adult education, vocational-technical education, community college services, and public service commissions have a vested interest in quality community college instruction. Further, they have development funds to help pay for it. Colleges must take the leadership in identifying areas of common interest and selling these boards and agencies on cooperative development. The result will be broadened resources and increased coordination and both will prove valuable in the current decade.

Colleges that embark on the eight-step journey described in this chapter are not guaranteed success in meeting the challenges of the 1980s. They will, however, have designed a unified model for engaging them. Part-time faculty are an integral part of this model. In 1973 O'Banion stated the goal of staff development. Eight years later his words remain valid and compelling in fostering part-time faculty development. "Unless the priority of the future is placed on people — the people who staff the people's college — the community college we know now may cease to exist and the community college we dream of may never come to be" (1974, p. 40).

References

Cross, K. P. "Old Practices and New Purposes." *Community and Junior College Journal,* 50 (1), 4.

Koltai, L., and Erickson, L. G. "Statesmanship and Survival." *Community and Junior College Journal, 50* (4), 9.

O'Banion, T. "Staff Development: A Priority on Persons." In R. Yarrington (Ed.), *Educational Opportunity for All: New Staff for New Students.* Washington, D.C.: American Association of Community and Junior Colleges, 1974.

Michael H. Parsons is dean of instructional affairs at Hagerstown Junior College in Hagerstown, Maryland.

Further resources from the ERIC Clearinghouse for Junior Colleges can provide examples on how community colleges are effectively using their part-time staff.

Sources and Information: Using Part-Time Faculty Effectively

Donna Sillman

This concluding chapter highlights the Educational Resources Information Center's (ERIC) references concerning part-time faculty, who now represent over 50 percent of the total teaching faculty in community colleges (Friedlander, 1978). The trend of hiring more part-time instructors is seen by Lombardi (1975) as a consequence of increasing numbers of part-time students, movement toward off-campus classes in scattered locations, and growing numbers of unemployed college graduates with teaching majors.

There are definite advantages to the employment of instructors on a part-time basis. Students have the opportunity to study their field of interest, however narrow it may be, under outstanding people whose primary employment may be in industry or other postsecondary institutions. Colleges can respond more effectively to community needs while keeping their budgets in tow (Guichard and others, 1975; Price and Lane, 1976). In addition to curricular flexibility, Marsh and Lamb (1975) add these factors to the list of advantages for institutions: scheduling flexibility, potential savings — one-third per course, part-time faculty cost less than the price of full-time faculty — and discouragement of collective bargaining due to factionalization of the faculty. For instructors, Koltai (1976) adds the opportunity to use part-time employment as a means of beginning a career in postsecondary teaching.

There are, however, problems. Marsh and Lamb (1975) reported a compilation by the Napa College Part-Time Teachers Association. Lack of formal hiring procedures leading to a failure of affirmative action and arbitrary firings, no long-term commitment to the institution, unresponsive teaching resulting from inadequate evaluation and little provision for student contact, over-representation by administration in the employment relation, and low faculty morale were cited as drawbacks in part-time staffing.

Part-time-employment issues in California community colleges were studied by Guichard and others (1975) and Petersen and others (1976). It was found that despite legislative attempts to clarify the law concerning employment of certificated personnel in community colleges, inappropriate or inconsistent language still existed for temporary and part-time personnel. Opinions concerning proportional benefits part-time instructors should receive (particularly in the areas of tenure, salary, fringe benefits, and participation in campus affairs) differed greatly. In a report to the state Board of Governors of Community Colleges, the authors recommended that legislation to mandate prorata pay or provide tenure for part-time faculty be opposed and that the question of due process in relation to the provisions of the Education Code concerning temporary and part-time faculty be considered. The results of sixteen California legal decisions in cases involving the status or status and pay of part-time faculty in California community colleges were reported by Plosser and Hammel (1976).

The level of participation of part-timers in the governing structure was studied by Bennett and Shannon (1976). They found that part-time faculty at the downtown campus of Florida Junior College felt their say in school policy was almost non-existent. Ferris (1976) reported a similar situation in the Los Rios District. Desmarais and Wiggins (1975) cited what could be two exemplary structures of shared-authority.

Cohen (1976) points to the tendency of full-time instructors to ignore part-time faculty in their own fields. Relegation to evening and outreach classes and neither step-increments despite years of service nor fringe benefits for their participation in committee work, curriculum development, counseling, and department meetings have been added to the list (Ferris, 1976).

The exclusion of part-time faculty from the bargaining unit is also a concern. In a survey of over 6,000 faculty, trustees, students, presidents, and administrators about faculty relations in the Washington State Community College System (*Community College Faculty Collective Bargaining . . . ,* 1975) 70.6 percent of respondents favored including part-time faculty in the bargaining unit. An analysis of 139 negotiated faculty contracts was conducted by the Bernard Baruch College National Center for the Study of Collective Bargaining in Higher Education (*Part-Time Faculty in 2-Year Colleges,* 1977). The contracts described part-time faculty in a variety of ways and often included restrictions on the number or percentages of part-time faculty which could be hired. Approximately one half of the contracts did not include part-time faculty as members of the unit. Part-timers generally received less job security than regular faculty, less compensation, and fewer benefits. The inclusion question is also explored by Hankin (1979) who looked at higher education collective bargaining after it has reached litigation.

Part-Time Faculty Characteristics

A number of people have broken down attributes of part-time faculty members. Grymes (1976) surveyed the part-time instructors at J. Sargeant Reynolds Community College on the following: age, race, sex, educational background, and previous teaching experience; whether or not they were generally satisfied with their association with the college; whether or not they were employed elsewhere and, if so, in what field; their primary reasons for teaching at the college; whether they were receiving adequate support and assistance; the extent to which they were available to students for counseling and advising; and whether or not they wanted to become involved in college and/or divisional activities.

At Johnson County Community College (JCCC), Quanty (1976) drew the following profile. Of the respondents, 56 percent were male and 97 percent were white. Their average age was thirty-three. The master's degree was held by 54 percent while 15 percent had more advanced degrees. Part-time instructors taught an average of 1.5 classes but 60 percent taught only one class. Further, 53 percent had taught at JCCC for less than two years; outside jobs were held by 87 percent; and 55 percent said they would accept full-time positions if offered. Although 95 percent were satisfied with other aspects of their employment, only 65 percent were satisfied with their salaries.

In a study conducted at fifteen community colleges in California, Sewell and others (1976) found that over 90 percent of part-time instructors work either full or part time in another capacity. Their average hourly pay ranges from $11.25 to $14.56 with an average load of 4.5 hours. Another California study (*Community College Instructors' Out-of-Class Professional Functions* . . . , 1978) reported that 77.9 percent of the part-time faculty had seven or less years of teaching experience at community colleges. Nearly 23 percent were working solely at the college and over 50 percent wanted to obtain full-time positions. Part-time faculty with greater teaching loads participated in more functions, and a positive relationship existed between desire for full-time employment and out-of-class participation.

Friedlander (1979) compared data from three nationwide surveys to determine the difference in instructional practices of part-time and full-time instructors. Part-timers were found to have less teaching experience, to have taught fewer years at their current institutions, and to hold lower academic credentials. They had less choice in the selection of course materials, assigned fewer pages to read, used less instructional media, recommended or required fewer out-of-class activities, and placed less emphasis on written assignments in determining student grades. In terms of professional development, they read fewer scholarly journals, were less likely to be members of or attend meetings of professional associations, and were less likely to request release time. They were, however, more likely to express a need for interaction with colleagues and administrators. In a review of the literature, Lombardi (1976) discussed the academic preparation and experience of part-time faculty.

The satisfaction of part-time humanities instructors was studied by Obetz (1976). Only 16 percent of her sample was highly satisfied. The dissatisfied part-time faculty member was less likely to be employed full time in an additional job and strongly supported collective bargaining. For them opportunities to be creative were limited, salaries inadequate, and job security non-existent. Cohen and Brawer (1977) used results of a national survey to examine the characteristics of part-time humanities instructors.

Abel (1976) described the part-time instructors at Santa Monica College as committed to their profession but prohibited from full-time jobs by the employment crisis. Their qualifications compared well with those of full-time faculty and they invested a substantial amount of time in preparation for class. Their low college salaries are a large proportion of their total income and many hold multiple assignments at various educational institutions. They are aggrieved by low salaries, lack of fringe benefits, and low status. Most would accept a full-time job, but significantly half would prefer to remain part time if their pay and status were improved. They are denied the opportunity to prove themselves and then penalized for failure to demonstrate their merit. The high proportion of women in this group could be considered an example of the discriminatory treatment of women in academe.

Salaries

Pay for part-time faculty varies greatly. Lombardi (1975) discusses the three major methods of payment—hour rate, semester rate, and prorata based on the full-time-instructors' salary schedule. He also predicts a trend toward increasing salaries (1976a). The pay of part-time instructors teaching lecture classes in California was studied by Hopper (1973). In a report written for college boards and administrators of California community colleges, the cost of converting from part time to prorata scales and prorata cost comparisons for 30- , 25- , and 15-hour work weeks was determined (*Preliminary Report on Part-Time Faculty*, 1975).

Brown and Romoser (1976) surveyed thirty-seven two-year institutions across the country and compared faculty compensation in 1973–74 to that in 1975–76. An 8.2 percent increase was found with an average part-time rate of $158 per quarter-hour. Data on part-time teaching salaries in county colleges were tabulated by the New Jersey State Department of Higher Education (*Financial Report of the County Colleges* . . . , 1978). In 1978 Illinois part-time faculty rates per semester hour averaged $238 while overload rates were $362 (*Faculty and Administrative Salaries* . . . , 1978).

Recruitment and Orientation

Bender and Breuder (1973) reviewed policies for part-timers in those institutions in which they were a majority of instructors. The study revealed few colleges had developed appropriate plans for selecting, orienting, training, servicing, or supervising their part-time faculty. However, the growing number of part-time faculty has directed more attention to these activities.

Kennedy (1966) studied Illinois and Maryland state policies on recruitment of part-time junior college teachers and institutional practices of recruitment, sources and techniques. The sources and qualifications of part-time faculty in general were reviewed by Lombardi (1975). This was followed by a study specific to non-campus colleges (1977). In the Hagerstown Junior College (Maryland) systems model of adjunct faculty development, Harris and Parsons (1975) cite recruitment as the first phase of their program. Handbooks or manuals as one means of orienting new part-timers has become more widely used (*Part-Time Faculty Handbook, 1975–76*, 1975; Harris and Parsons, 1975; Palmer, 1979; *Part-Time Faculty Handbook*, 1976; *This Book . . . ,* 1977; Watson, 1977; *Clark Technical College . . . ,* 1977; *Community College of Vermont . . . ,* 1979). Handbooks cover such topics as college history, philosophy, objectives, and academic standards; responsibilities and benefits of part-time faculty status; college procedures; academic regulations; format for proposing changes in academic regulations; college facilities, special equipment, and services; organizational flow chart; student and instructor rights; description of the faculty; presidents' philosophy of administration; glossary of terms for administrative style; continuing education; community services academic and technical-vocational programs; nondiscrimination clause; child development program; volunteers; college/community events; college calendar; curriculum development and instructional support; annotated bibliography of the college's reports and basic reading materials on adult development and learning, competence-based and experiential learning, and instructional development. Behm and others (1977) suggest an outline for formulating a resource book to be used as the basis of a comprehensive development system.

Staff Development

Staff development has been a major concern in community colleges for the last decade, however, only in the last few years has there been a real interest in development programs for part-time faculty. In 1975 Moe (1977) surveyed the deans of instruction in all community colleges with enrollment of over five thousand. The following types of development activities were found: orientation, division meetings, liaison with full-time instructors, workshops, newsletters, seminars, professional-development libraries, videotape evaluation of instruction, and funds for training outside the college.

After reviewing current development efforts, Behm and others (1977) categorized them into five models, but they focused on one complex model. It proposes a school gain administrative and financial support, establish direct lines of communication between part- and full-time faculty, and provide a resource book, workshops, and lead-instructor system.

A handbook for the professional development of part-time faculty was created by Weichenthal and others (1977). Divided into five sections, it contains information that includes a planning guide, a descriptive approach to needs-assessment, the evaluation of programs and activities, a plan for supervision of part-time faculty members, and programs, resources, and services useful to professional development.

Grymes (1977) suggested that varied methods be used to present material and that seminars and workshops should feature community as well as institutional representatives. Part-timers should be made part of the institution so thay they will actively share in planning and implementation of the institution's instructional program. Open and effective channels of communication, coordination, and cooperation are thought essential.

Schafer (1976) suggests a model of training that includes an orientation program each term, continuous problem-solving sessions, a faculty handbook, and a rotating schedule that would make administrators available for evening meetings. As a result of an extensive survey of selected two-year college administrators and adjunct faculty, Fent (1979) developed a model for a semester-long development program and suggested that it be conducted twice weekly for maximum participation.

The following colleges have descriptions of their part-time-faculty development programs in the ERIC collection: Burlington County College, New Jersey (Hammons, Wallace, and Watts, 1978); Eastfield College, Texas (Moe, 1977); Hagerstown Junior College, Maryland (Harris and Parsons, 1975; Parsons, 1978); Maricopa Community College District, Arizona (Hoover, 1976); Mount Hood Community College, Oregon (Justice, 1976); Mount San Jacinto College, California (Lombardi, 1976b; Nelson, 1978); Pima Community College, Arizona (Schultz and Roed, 1978); Richland College, Texas (Hammons, Wallace, and Watts, 1978); Seminole Community College, Florida (Elwood, 1976); St. Petersburg Junior College, Florida (Long, 1978; Fellows, 1975); West Virginia Northern Community College, West Virginia (Persinger, 1977); and William Rainey Harper College, Illinois (Voegel and Lucas, 1977).

Supervision and Evaluation

Supervision and evaluation of part-time staff were studied by Heinberg (1966), Falk (1975), and Fellows (1975). Administrators from sixty-three California junior colleges were surveyed by Heinberg (1966) to determine (1) who is responsible for the improvement of the part-time instructional staff in evening programs, (2) how the staff is and should be supervised and evaluated, and (3) how to develop practices for evaluation and improvement. The study lists the practices most highly recommended.

The similarities and differences in perceptions among full- and part-time community college business instructors and their supervisors in selected Illinois public community colleges was investigated by Falk (1975). Fellows (1975) prepared and tested an evaluation plan for part-time continuing education faculty that included a pre-teaching, self-instructional booklet on concepts of adult education, self-evaluation by faculty after completing their teaching assignment, and personal coaching sessions with administrators to identify needs and strategies for improvements. Significant growth was indicated.

References

The ERIC documents (ED numbers) listed, unless otherwise indicated, are available on microfiche (MF), or in paper copy (PC) from the ERIC Document Reproduction Service (EDRS), Computer Microfilm International Corporation, P.O. Box 190, Arlington, Va. 22210. The MF price for documents under 480 pages is $0.83. Prices for PC are: 1–25 pages, $1.82; 26–50 pages, $3.32; 51–75 pages, $4.82; 76–100 pages, $6.32. For materials having more than 100 pages, add $1.50 for each 25-page increment (or fraction thereof). Postage must be added to all orders. Abstracts of these and other documents in the junior college collection are available upon request from the ERIC Clearinghouse for Junior Colleges, Room 96, Powell Library, University of California, Los Angeles, CA 90024. Bracketed publication dates are approximate.

Abel, E. K. *Invisible and Indispensable: Part-Time Teachers in California Community Colleges.* Unpublished paper, [1976]. 58pp. (ED 132 984)
Behm, R., and others. *Accentuating the Professional Role of Part-Time Faculty.* Unpublished paper, [1977]. 11pp. (ED 143 401)
Bender, L. W., and Breuder, R. L. "Part-Time Teachers—'Step Children' of the Community College." *Community College Review,* 1973, *1* (1), 29–37.

Bennett, D., and Shannon, M. L. *A Study to Determine the Involvement in Governance of Part-time Instructional Personnel at the Downtown Campus of Florida Junior College at Jacksonville.* Unpublished paper, 1976. 20pp. (ED 129 389)

Brown, B., and Romoser, R. C. *Part-Time Faculty Salary Rates 1973*–74 and 1975–76 for Selected Community Colleges. Cleveland, Ohio: Cuyahoga Community College, 1976. 8pp. (ED 121 370)

Clark Technical College Adjunct Faculty Handbook. Springfield, Ohio: Clark Technical College, [1977]. 46pp. (ED 144 647)

Cohen, A. M. "The Faculty Member as Recluse." Speech presented at the 7th Annual International Institute on the Community College, Sarnia, Ontario, Canada, June 14–16. 19pp. (ED 125 681)

Cohen, A. M., and Brawer, F. B. *The Two-Year College Instructor Today.* New York: Praeger, 1977. (Available from Praeger Special Studies, 200 Park Avenue, New York, New York 10017, $16.50)

Community College Faculty Collective Bargaining: Report and Recommendations of the Advisory Committee on Community College Faculty Collective Bargaining to the Senate Select Committee. Olympia: Washington State Legislature, 1975. 63pp. (ED 111 470)

Community College Instructors' Out-of-Class Professional Functions: Report of a Survey of Full-Time and Part-Time Faculty in California Community Colleges. Sacramento: California Community and Junior College Association, 1978. 61pp. (ED 154 873)

Community College of Vermont Staff Manual for Learning Support Staff. Montpelier: Community College of Vermont, 1979. 106pp. (ED 175 492)

Desmarais, A., and Wiggins, E. F. *A Proposed Participatory Governance Structure for the Division of Continuing Education and Community Services at Bristol Community College.* Unpublished paper, 1975. 71pp. (ED 103 032)

Elwood, W. F., Jr. *The Development of a Curriculum for a Community College Teaching Workshop for Adjunct Faculty.* Sanford, Fla.: Seminole Community College, 1976. 29pp. (ED 129 395)

Faculty and Administrative Salaries in the Public Community Colleges of Illinois 1977–78. Data and Characteristics, Vol. 6. Springfield: Illinois Community College Board, 1978. 58pp. (ED 151 041 — Available in microfiche only)

Falk, C. F. *A Study of the In-Service Education and Supervision Needs of Community College Business Instructors in the State of Illinois.* Unpublished paper, 1975. 42pp. (ED 130 710)

Fellows, D. B. "An Evaluation Plan for Part-Time Faculty in Community/Junior Colleges." Unpublished doctoral dissertation, Nova University, 1975. 164pp. (ED 133 009)

Fent, J. E. "Professional Development for Adjunct Faculty in Michigan Community Colleges." Unpublished doctoral dissertation, Walden University, 1979. 184pp. (ED 172 855) — Available in microfiche only)

Ferris, P. *The Part-Time Instructor in the Los Rios District: An Analysis.* Sacramento, Calif.: Los Rios Community College District, 1976. 14pp. (ED 121 364)

Financial Report of the County Colleges of the State of New Jersey for the Fiscal Year Ended June 30, 1977. Trenton: New Jersey State Department of Higher Education, 1978. 129pp. (ED 151 045)

Friedlander, J. *Using the Talents of Part-Time Faculty. Junior College Resource Review.* Los Angeles: ERIC Clearinghouse for Junior Colleges, 1978. 6pp. (ED 162 706)

Friedlander, J. "Instructional Practices of Part-Time Faculty in Community Colleges." Paper presented at the 19th annual forum of the Association for Institutional Research San Diego, Calif., May 13–17, 1979. 23pp. (ED 169 971)

Grymes, R. J., Jr. *A Survey and Analysis of Part-Time Instructors at J. Sargeant Reynolds Community College.* Richmond, Va.: J. Sargeant Reynolds Community College, 1976. 54pp (ED 125 687)

Grymes, R. J., Jr. *Staff Development for Adjunct Faculty.* Unpublished paper, [1977]. 15pp. (ED 148 409)

Guichard, G., and others. *Part-Time Employment, Item 8.* Sacramento: California Community Colleges, Office of the Chancellor, 1975. 23pp. (ED 111 464—Available in microfiche only)

Hammons, J., Wallace, T. H. S., and Watts, G. *Staff Development in the Community College: A Handbook.* Topical Paper No. 66. Los Angeles, ERIC Clearinghouse for Junior Colleges, 1978. 74pp. (ED 154 887)

Hankin, J. N. "Unit Determination: Basic Criteria in Federal and State Jurisdictions. Trends in Exclusion of Supervisory and Managerial Personnel, Faculty in Professional Schools, Multi-Campus Units, Support Professionals, Part-Time Personnel and Others." Paper presented at the annual meeting of the National Center for the Study of Collective Bargaining in Higher Education, April 23, 1979. 24pp. (ED 172 898)

Harris, D. A., and Parsons, M. H. *Adjunct Faculty: A Working System of Development.* Hagerstown Junior College, 1975. 12pp. (ED 115 318)

Heinberg, S. "Procedures for the Supervision and Evaluation of New Part-Time Evening-Division Instructors in California Junior Colleges." Unpublished doctoral dissertation, University of Southern California, 1966. (Available from University Microfilms, 300 North Zeeb Road, Ann Arbor, Michigan 48106, Order No. 67-405)

Hoover, V. D. "Maricopa County Community College District Training and Staff Development Program for Part-Time Occupational Instructors." In C. R. Doty and R. Gepner (Eds.), *Post-Secondary Personnel Development.* Vol. 2. Proceedings of the National Conference on Personnel Development for Post Secondary Vocational and Technical Education Prgrams of Less than Baccalaureate Degree, St. Louis, Mo., January 18–21, 1976. 338pp. (ED 131 892)

Hopper, F. L. *A Study of the Policy of Hourly Wages for Part-time Instructors of Community Colleges in California.* Unpublished paper, 1973. 15pp. (ED 094 812)

Justice, P. *A Comprehensive Plan for Institutional Staff Development.* Final Project Report. Gresham, Oregon: Mount Hood Community College, 1976. 51pp. (ED 126 988)

Kennedy, G. J. "A Study of the Recruitment and Orientation Policies and Practices for Part-Time Instructors in the Public Junior Colleges of Illinois and Maryland." Unpublished doctoral dissertation, University of Maryland, 1966. (Available from University Microfilms, 300 North Zeeb Road, Ann Arbor, Michigan 48106, Order No. 67-6122)

Kennedy, G. J. "Preparation, Orientation, Utilization and Acceptance of Part-Time Instructors." *Junior College Journal,* 1967, *37* (7), 14–15.

Koltai, L. "The Part-time Faculty and the Community College." Speech presented at the Conference on Part-Time Teachers, Inglewood, Calif., January 28, 1976. 7pp. (ED 118 174)

Lombardi, J. *Part-Time Faculty in Community Colleges.* Topical Paper No. 54. Los Angeles: ERIC Clearinghouse for Junior Colleges, 1975. 62pp. (ED 115 316)

Lombardi, J. "Salaries for Part-Time Faculty: New Trends. An ERIC Review." *Community College Review,* 1976a, *3* (3), 77–88.

Lombardi, J. (Comp.) *Staff Development Programs for Part-Time Occupational-Vocational Instructors: An ERIC Brief.* Los Angeles: ERIC Clearinghouse for Junior Colleges, 1976b. 18pp. (ED 116 732)

Lombardi, J. *Noncampus Colleges: New Governance Patterns for Outreach Programs.* Topical Paper No. 60. Los Angeles: ERIC Clearinghouse for Junior Colleges, 1977. 80pp. (ED 136 880)

Long, E. J., Jr. "Analysis of Professional Development Needs of Part-Time Continuing Education Instructors at St. Petersburg Junior College." Unpublished doctoral dissertation, Nova University, 1978. 98pp. (ED 162 678)

Marsh, J. P., and Lamb, T. (Eds.), *An Introduction to Part-time Teaching Situations with Particular Emphasis on Its Impact at Napa Community College.* Unpublished paper, 1975. 46pp. (ED 125 683—Available in microfiche only)

Moe, J. "A Staff Development Model for Part-Time Instructors." In T. O'Banion (Ed.), *New Directions for Community Colleges: Developing Staff Potential*, no. 19. San Francisco: Jossey-Bass, Inc., 433 California Street, San Francisco, CA 94104, $5.95)

Nelson, H. E. *Competency-Based Teacher Education for Community College Instructors: A Partly Self-Instructional Staff Development Program.* San Jacinto, Calif.: Mount San Jacinto College, 1978. 16pp. (ED 158 829—Also available from the Multimedia Office, Mt. San Jacinto College, 21400 Highway 79, San Jacinto, CA 92383)

Obetz, R. "The Part-Time Humanities Instructor." In S. H. Schlesinger (Ed.), *The Humanities in Two-Year Colleges: Faculty Characteristics.* Los Angeles: Center for the Study of Community Colleges and ERIC Clearinghouse for Junior Colleges, 1976. 71pp. (ED 130 721)

Palmer, A. *Associate Faculty Handbook.* Holbrook, Ariz.: Northland Pioneer College, 1979. 37pp. (ED number not yet assigned)

Parsons, M. H. "Part-Time Faculty: A Statewide Model for Development." Paper presented at the Northeast Regional Conference of the National Council for Staff, Program and Organizational Development, Mt. Laurel, N.J., November 17, 1978. 14pp. (ED 161 484)

Part-Time Faculty Handbook. Texas City, Texas: College of the Mainland, [1976]. 39pp. (ED 136 894)

Part-Time Faculty Handbook, 1975-76. Rockville, Md.: Montgomery College. [1976]. 60pp. (ED 112 980)

Part-Time Faculty in 2-Year Colleges. New York: Bernard Baruch College, National Center for the Study of Collective Bargaining in Higher Education, City University of New York, 1977. 6pp. (ED 144 650)

Persinger, G. R. *Professional Development for Part-Time Faculty.* Research and Demonstration Project. Wheeling, Va.: Council for North Central Community and Junior Colleges, 1977. 89pp. (ED 168 664)

Petersen, A. L., and others. *Legislation and Part-Time Employment.* Sacramento: California Community Colleges, 1976. 60pp. (ED 134 256)

Plosser, W. D., and Hammel, J. H. *Temporary, Contract, or Regular? A Report About Court Cases Involving the Issues of the Status and Pay of Part-Time Faculty in California Community Colleges.* Sacramento: California Community and Junior College Association, 1976. 102pp. (ED 133 015—Also available from California Community and Junior College Association, 2017 "O" Street, Sacramento, Calif. 95814, $3.50)

Preliminary Report on Part-Time Faculty. Sacramento: California Community Colleges, 1975. 8pp. (ED 105 930)

Price, F. H., and Lane, W. H. *An Analysis of Community and Junior College Use of Part-Time Faculty.* Unpublished paper, 1976. 17pp. (ED 121 362)

Quanty, M. *Part-Time Instructor Survey.* Overland Park, Kans.: Johnson County Community College, 1976. 24pp. (ED 127 000)

Schafer, M. I. "The Forgotten Faculty. Staff Development for Part-Time Occupational Instructors in Post-Secondary Education." In C. R. Doty and R. Gepner (Eds.), *Post-Secondary Personnel Development.* Vol. 1. Proceedings of the National Conference on Personnel Development for Post Secondary Vocational and Technical Education Programs of Less than Baccalaureate Degree, St. Louis, Mo., January 18–21, 1976. 496pp. (ED 131 891)

Schultz, R. E., and Roed, W. J. *Report on Inservice Needs of Community College Part-Time Occupational Instructors.* Tuscon: College of Education, Arizona University, 1978. 29pp. (ED 156 290)

Sewell, D. H., and others. *Report on a Statewide Survey About Part-Time Faculty in California Community Colleges.* Sacramento: California Community and Junior College Association, 1976. 40pp. (ED 118 195)

This Book Is for the Use and Enlightenment of Tanana Valley Community College Part-Time Instruc-

tors. Fairbanks, Alaska: Tanana Valley Community College, [1977]. 74pp. (ED 152 355)

Voegel, G. H., and Lucas, J. A. *Evaluation of 1976*-1977 Faculty Development Program. Vol. 9 no. 4. Palatine, Ill.: William Rainey Harper College, 1977. 30pp. (ED 145 880)

Watson, R. J. *Developing a Continuing Education Office: Two Important Documents*. Baltimore County, Md.: Essex Community College, [1977]. 59pp. (ED 148 416)

Weichenthal, P. B., and others. *Professional Development Handbook for Community College Part-Time Faculty Members*. Urbana: College of Education and Office of Continuing Education and Public Services, University of Illinois, 1977. 142pp. (ED 156 288)

Donna Sillman is bibliographer at the ERIC Clearinghouse for Junior Colleges.

Index

101

New Directions Quarterly Sourcebooks

New Directions for Community Colleges is one of several distinct series of quarterly sourcebooks published by Jossey-Bass. The sourcebooks in each series are designed to serve both as *convenient compendiums* of the latest knowledge and practical experience on their topics and as *long-life reference tools.*

One-year, four-sourcebook subscriptions for each series cost $18 for individuals (when paid by personal check) and $30 for institutions, libraries, and agencies. Single copies of earlier sourcebooks are available at $6.95 each *prepaid* (or $7.95 each when *billed*).

A complete listing is given below of current and past sourcebooks in the *New Directions for Community Colleges* series. The titles and editors-in-chief of the other series are also listed. To subscribe, or to receive further information, write: New Directions Subscriptions, Jossey-Bass Inc., Publishers, 433 California Street, San Francisco, California 94104.

New Directions for Community Colleges
Arthur M. Cohen, Editor-in-Chief
Florence B. Brawer, Associate Editor

1973: 1. *Toward a Professional Faculty,* Arthur M. Cohen
2. *Meeting the Financial Crisis,* John Lombardi
3. *Understanding Diverse Students,* Dorothy Knoell
4. *Updating Occupational Education,* Norman Harris
1974: 5. *Implementing Innovative Instruction,* Roger Garrison
6. *Coordinating State Systems,* Edmund Gleazer, Roger Yarrington
7. *From Class to Mass Learning,* William Birenbaum
8. *Humanizing Student Services,* Clyde Blocker
1975: 9. *Using Instructional Technology,* George Voegel
10. *Reforming College Governance,* Richard Richardson
11. *Adjusting to Collective Bargaining,* Richard Ernst
12. *Merging the Humanities,* Leslie Koltai
1976: 13. *Changing Managerial Perspectives,* Barry Heermann
14. *Reaching Out Through Community Service,* Hope Holcomb
15. *Enhancing Trustee Effectiveness,* Victoria Dziuba, William Meardy
16. *Easing the Transition from Schooling to Work,* Harry Silberman, Mark Ginsburg

New Directions for Child Development
William Damon, Editor-in-Chief

New Directions for College Learning Assistance
Kurt V. Lauridsen, Editor-in-Chief

New Directions for Continuing Education
Alan B. Knox, Editor-in-Chief

New Directions for Exceptional Children
James G. Gallagher, Editor-in-Chief

New Directions for Experiential Learning
Morris T. Keeton and Pamela J. Tate, Editors-in-Chief

New Directions for Higher Education
JB Lon Hefferlin, Editor-in-Chief

New Directions for Institutional Advancement
A. Westley Rowland, Editor-in-Chief